"*Deconstructing* is invaluable for anyone ready to break through the walls that separate us from those who do not look like, love like, and believe like we do. What's at stake is the very survival of our democracy."   —Barbara Becker, author of *Heartwood: The Art of Living with the End in Mind*

"This book is an essential guide for anyone standing on the edge of their religion, wondering if there is a better way laying just beyond the boundaries of their faith. Rev Karla is the perfect guide to lead us through the journey of deconstructing toxic religion and constructing a life-giving faith."   —Rev. Brandan Robertson, TikTok pastor and author

"Rev Karla's *Deconstructing* offers pastoral and prophetic guidance for anyone moving beyond restrictive religious structures and into a more authentic and alive spiritual life. Her stories and insights bring wisdom, courage, and healing to those embarking on the journey of demolishing, repairing, and restoring their faith."   —Ben Katt, author of *The Way Home*

"As spiritual teacher and leader in metaphysics, I appreciate Rev Karla's courageous journey in deconstructing the life-limiting indoctrination as taught by most Christian religions. Due to the bulk of their tenets, a whole beautiful and powerful sect of individuals (women) are left out, unseen, and unappreciated. Kudos to Rev Karla for this brilliant work."   —Rev. Dr. Michelle Wadleigh, author of *Shadow Work*

"Rev Karla's book is a beacon guiding home those feeling lost in a spiritual wilderness. She honors the places one feels broken and gently navigates the reader towards mending those spaces. *Deconstructing* gives the reader permission to be curious, explore their spiritual boundaries, and step into their authenticity. It's honest, heartfelt, and beautiful."
—Stephanie Jo Warren, podcast host, educator, author

"[Kamstra] has brilliantly addressed the complex process of deconstructing with clarity. She makes one's own personal journey appear to be possible and simpler to begin, to navigate, and to accept with confirmation. . . . A trail is blazed through Karla's spiritual wilderness for others to follow. . . . She empowers our inner strength and confidence to experience a journey outside and beyond the church. . . . This book is freeing."
—Tom Porter, founder and
president of Malibu Wellness

"*Deconstructing* is a moving and intimate personal account of demolishing, repairing, and restoring faith. There are a lot of folks out there who can criticize the Bible and the church, and who can speak endlessly about deconstruction, and Rev Karla can hang with the best of them, but she offers something that others cannot: a map and a model for bringing the pieces back together to reconstruct a richer, a deeper, and a more enduring faith. A large portion of the deconstruction community has been asking for a resource just like this, and it will no doubt be an indispensable guide for many through the mental and emotional labor of leaving church to find faith." —Dan McClellan, Bible scholar, author, and social media personality

Deconstructing

Deconstructing

LEAVING CHURCH,
FINDING FAITH

Karla Kamstra

ST. MARTIN'S
ESSENTIALS
NEW YORK

First published in the United States by St. Martin's Essentials, an imprint of
St. Martin's Publishing Group

www.stmartins.com

Library of Congress Cataloging-in-Publication Data

Names: Kamstra, Karla, author.
Title: Deconstructing : leaving church, finding faith / Karla Kamstra.
Description: First edition. | New York, NY : St. Martin's Essentials, 2024. |
    Includes bibliographical references. |
Identifiers: LCCN 2024025315 | ISBN 9781250292759 (hardcover) |
    ISBN 9781250292766 (ebook)
Subjects: LCSH: Women in Christianity. | Feminist theology. |
    Patriarchy—Religious life—Christianity. | Spiritual life. | Faith.
Classification: LCC BV639.W7 K365 2024 | DDC 270.082—dc23/
    eng/20240618
LC record available at https://lccn.loc.gov/2024025315

Our books may be purchased in bulk for promotional, educational, or business
use. Please contact your local bookseller or the Macmillan Corporate and
Premium Sales Department at 1-800-221-7945, extension 5442, or by email at
MacmillanSpecialMarkets@macmillan.com.

First Edition: 2024

10   9   8   7   6   5   4   3   2   1

She said, "What does it mean to be an ordained Elder for the Presbyterian Church?"

I said, "Well Grandma. It means I'm chosen to help lead and shepherd the congregation."

Pause.

I said, "What do you think of that?"

She said, "Well as long as it brings you closer to God. . . ."

She let that sentence hang there, because that was the space between her generation and mine.

Between her beliefs and mine.

She's long gone.

But that sentence still holds meaning for me and my journey of deconstructing, leaving church, and finding my faith.

Because this journey has indeed brought me closer to God.

And somehow, some way, she knows that.

This book is in honor of the grandmother who planted the seed of spirituality in my life.

She is the reason you are reading this book.

I'm forever grateful.

CONTENTS

How Did I End Up Here?

Beloved, you are not alone.

If you found your way here because you are untangling from your indoctrinated religious beliefs, those words may do little to comfort you.

Rest assured, I understand this. I have been right where you are. I wanted to believe that others would arrive to help me on this healing journey to reclaim my spirituality and to heal what organized religion had taken from me. I wanted to believe that others understood and that I was not alone.

Except . . . I was alone.

I was facing the stark reality that nothing about my life inside church prepared me for life outside of it. Of course, it wouldn't have. Church needed me to stay rooted inside its structure, obedient to its dogma, and submissive to its authority. Its own survival depended on that. A member who will not submit to this structure is a threat to it.

There is no compromise: submit or leave.

I left.

Yes, this was the loneliness of my own doing. I had the choice to stay, faking it in the pews by spiritually "checking out." I had witnessed people who had done that for many years, so why couldn't I? Why wasn't it enough for me to be the "good Christian"—a phrase that was never used but fundamentally understood to mean be silent, obedient, and never, ever challenge church authority? Why couldn't I just show up to church, study my Bible, pay my tithe, raise my hands in praise at the appropriate time, and then go home until next Sunday?

That's Christianity on autopilot. Lather. Rinse. Repeat. This may work for some, but not for me. It simply wasn't in my DNA to be that type of Christian.

What wasn't clear then but would eventually become clear to me was that I myself was not the problem—it was the church's rules that dictated what it meant to be a good Christian that were the problem.

The rules.

Some may call it dogma. Others theology. Whatever you call it, it always felt restrictive. Those rules felt like they kept God in a box that was too small. And I had literally spent a lifetime trying to contort myself and become small enough to fit into that box as well.

It was as suffocating as it sounds, and I finally realized that it was this God box from which I needed to escape.

It was time to release God from those rules. This book will share my journey from silent obedience to living a spiritually empowered life.

Those are the bookends, and a lifetime of wisdom, heartache, wonder, and surprise are contained herein.

Beloved, what about you?

Do you feel a deep void that church can no longer fill—an emptiness in your heart and soul that simply will not abate, no matter what you do? Even if you have go-to spiritual practices of prayer, meditation, journaling, and the like, you can't shake the lingering sense that "something" is still missing from your life.

I've been there.

For years, I felt an emptiness in my heart and soul—a spiritual unrest—that I couldn't explain. When I tried to pinpoint the source of it, I always fell short. It frustrated me and convinced me that there was something wrong with my spirituality.

But I really tried. Can you relate?

I attended church. I listened intently to every word the pastor said. I overcommitted to activities and functions. I dove into my spiritual practices seeking meaning and clarity for what I was feeling.

And still, the need for something else would not leave my soul.

As I continued to struggle with the changes arising in me, I began to sense that my spiritual unrest was not going to go away until I discovered where it was coming from and what it meant for me outside of the Christianity I knew.

At first, the thought of moving away from my spiritual community to try to figure out what was happening terrified me. I was battling a lifetime of religious indoctrination* that taught me that seeking answers *outside* church was dangerous and sinful. (Terms marked with an asterisk appear in the glossary.) To do so literally meant my soul would be in peril. I was told the Bible held all the answers to life's questions—and if I wasn't clear about it, the next step was to ask my pastors.

The practice of seeking wisdom first from the Bible and then from your pastor is common within evangelical*/fundamentalist Christianity. While it *can* be helpful for people needing advice on issues of religion, I have witnessed and experienced for myself congregants being accused of "weak faith" for even acknowledging their internal stirrings. We were told we had "doubters' minds."

I have also seen the dark side of this belief system, where pastors inappropriately attempt to fill roles that belong to qualified therapists. I have heard them dismiss issues of mental health and admonish women for considering divorce from abusive husbands. I have even listened as young women shared their heartbreak for being told they weren't allowed to date other members of the church because the pastor didn't approve of these relationships. This is the same mentality and religious ideology I've seen speak of "praying the gay away."

Admittedly, my experience may shock some of you as you read about the depths of control and manipulation tactics utilized by church authorities to control their "flock." Then again, some of you may find it mild compared to your own experience. Christian doctrine varies so greatly that a Presbyterian and a Westboro Baptist Church–goer—both Christians—would be equally aghast at the other's services.

Even in congregations that seem more open-minded or "progressive," you may find yourself hesitant to share your feelings with anyone in your community. Within each denomination are unspoken "membership" rules that many fear breaking, lest they're seen as lacking faith or, even worse, fear repercussions for challenging the patriarchal structure upon which Christianity is built.

Still, the sheer number of people who are leaving Christianity indicates that many are like me—ready to answer the call to reclaim their spirituality outside the construct of their religious heritage. According to the data, for the first time in US history, church membership has fallen below 50 percent and continues to decline. This indicates that we are no longer a Christian nation.

I have the gift of hindsight, which shows me that the best thing I ever did for my spiritual journey was listen to my inner voice that beckoned me to dive into the unrest I was feeling. I began to covertly seek out other wisdom keepers whose teachings differed from the Christian theology I had known my entire life. As I studied and learned from these scholars, my feelings vacillated between relief, anger, confusion, fear, and clarity. I soaked up knowledge from teachers of many different backgrounds and beliefs. With each book I read and lecture I attended came new concepts that I had never heard before—challenging me, yet enriching and expanding my understanding of human spirituality.

Little by little, my spiritual unrest began to point me to my eventual path out of church as I increasingly came to rely on and identify with readings and teachings outside my Christian heritage. It was an interesting season to say the least. I continued to wear the façade of the good Christian and kept to myself the things I was learning: the additional text put in the Bible to change the original meaning, Christianity's dark history surrounding its use of torture and abuse as a way to control the masses, and, most importantly, I witnessed the way people around the world sought sacred meaning in their lives by honoring the Divine in ways that reflected their own traditions and cultures.

Still, off to church I would go to sing hymns of praise while secretly longing to return home and dive into the latest book by Bishop John Shelby Spong and other similar authors.

In other words, I was living a paradox, which for me meant that I was living two contradictory experiences at the same time. This was one of many paradoxes to come, and they had no end in sight—at least at that time. I couldn't see what my future in church looked like. I would experience similar things throughout my journey. I entered the spiritual wilderness* (a concept I explain in chapter 1), untangled from the beliefs inside my Christian faith that had become a weapon of control instead of a source of inspiration. I healed my religious trauma* and reclaimed my spirituality, and I now live a spiritually empowered life as a transformed, unchurched, nonconforming Christian* who honors the spiritual—but not religious—path.

Does this paradox sound familiar, Beloved? Do you find it difficult to describe what you are experiencing? That is not uncommon, because you have never been here before. Faith was most likely a stalwart. A shelter in a time of storm. So steadfast and reliable that it was the one thing you could lean on . . . until one day you simply couldn't.

Why? Because something shifted deep inside you, and there is no denying its presence, its pull, and the longing to discover its mysteries.

May I offer you some loving, gentle insight? It may be challenging to do so, but trust this process of deconstructing,* because this is indeed a sacred journey in which you are about to partake. You are answering the call to *demolish* the structure upon which your faith has been built, *repair* what religion may have done to you, and *restore* your heart and soul in a way that is authentically you.

Demolish. Repair. Restore.

These are what I believe are the steps to deconstructing one's faith. When you first begin the deconstructing journey—the process by which you untangle from the elements of your Christian heritage that have harmed you or no longer serve your highest good—it is not uncommon to sense a season of chaos in which:

- → the absence of religious structure feels messy and yet comforting;
- → the void left by your spiritual community feels lonely yet peaceful;
- → the lack of spiritual guidance from a church leader mandating "how" to be spiritual feels unsettling yet empowering; and
- → the loss of the container that had held your spirituality leaves you feeling vulnerable yet freed.

Yes, Beloved. Demolish. Repair. Restore.

There are two significant things to remember as you begin this journey of deconstructing.

The first is this: like anything in life that deals with profound change and paradigm shifts, this deconstructing process of demolishing, repairing, and restoring is not linear. You may spend months deconstructing what you learned in Bible school, then skip right to immersing yourself into teachings about Christian mysticism* or other world religions only to find yourself spiraling into anger as you begin to realize how much you have been emotionally and spiritually manipulated throughout your life. Or you may have a completely different process.

The second is that the deconstructing process doesn't have a timeline. I'm often asked by my followers how long they will be deconstructing. They're asking because this process can be challenging. It's life-changing. It rips the blinders off your reality. It shakes your foundational beliefs, and it often leaves you with the stark reality that those within your innermost circle should not be there.

In other words, you come face-to-face with your true self without the cloak of religious beliefs protecting you, and that can be intimidating and downright scary. I'm very sincere when I reply to those questions by saying that I do not know how long this deconstructing process will take for an individual, because I don't know. Every person's journey is different, and the path that takes you through deconstructing is just that—*your* path. It's all dependent upon your lived experiences, your religious heritage, your beliefs, and your willingness to face head-on what arrives and is asking for light, asking to be healed, and asking to be released.

I'll share my deconstructing journey that began years ago. Honestly, I'm still on this journey. I believe now that I always will be. That may not be what you wanted to hear, but I've never sugarcoated what deconstructing is. If I did, I would be no better than those church leaders who sought to control us through unethical, manipulative, and oftentimes egregious tactics.

One of the reasons that I believe people want a definitive timeline for deconstructing is because it takes us so far out of our comfort zones. Spirituality often packaged inside organized religion can feel comfy like an old cardigan that we can wrap ourselves in and snuggle in its warmth and familiarity. There isn't anything wrong with that. Spirituality should provide us with a sense of comfort and a sense of knowing that we are seen and loved.

There is another side to spirituality, however. That is the side that invites us to grow beyond conditioned beliefs that keep us in a silo with only people who look like, love like, and believe like we do. This silo type of spirituality convinces us of our spiritual superiority. We often exist in a religious culture so rigid that our loyalty to that culture is proven by how we judge others who exist outside our silo of faith.

Allowing this deconstruction journey of demolishing, repairing, and restoring to weave into our lives and our spirituality with no expectations or timelines invites an expansiveness into our spirituality in ways that we most likely did not have inside our religious experience. Even though I have been on this deconstructing journey for over thirteen years now, I am amazed and humbled by how often I am still greeted with new awareness and insight that helps me grow and expand my spiritual awakening in ways I never thought possible.

Even as I wrote this book, memories arrived that helped me build bridges back to childhood and to experiences inside church that were always pointing me to who I am today. If it weren't for being open to this deconstructing journey, I would have missed these healing moments.

I want that for you as well, Beloved.

Throughout this book, I'll share the stories of my deconstruction journey.

About my season of demolishing, when I began to untangle from my faith and found myself in the spiritual wilderness—the season when I felt most alone. I knew I could no longer pretend that something deep inside of me was questioning my faith and everything I knew about who—or even *what*—God is.

About how I began to repair the harm that modern American evangelical Christianity had caused. This was the season when I vowed that I would not be the victim in this story and that I would do the work to understand how powerful patriarchal religious structures create systems that demand loyalty and blind obedience.

About how my spirituality was restored in ways that I had not imagined when I first left church and entered the spiritual wilderness. Restoration for me looked like releasing the need for organized religion, finding the Holy in the everyday lived experiences, and equipping myself with the knowledge and tools to help others do the same.

Your deconstruction journey of demolishing, repairing, and restoring will look different, but there is power in our stories, and *Deconstructing* will offer you my story blended with the wisdom that I received along the way.

Deconstructing is my story about deconstructing from evangelical Christianity.

I share how I could no longer silence the inner voice that beckoned me to discover the Holy outside of my religious heritage, leading me to walk out of the church and never return.

And I demolished it all in a spectacular way. I abdicated from my leadership roles within church. I renounced beliefs that suffocated the rights of others. I relinquished the role of the good Christian, an unattainable and unsustainable title that I had chased my entire life. And I began to chip away at the religious foundation upon which all my beliefs, my identity, and my life had been built.

Demolishing meant I was an island, standing alone without my spiritual community that for years had loved and supported me.

If you feel as if you have experienced or will soon be experiencing a season of demolishing your religious heritage, this book is for you.

Each chapter is intentionally set up in a way to help you see yourself in my story, from entering the spiritual wilderness in chapter 1 to the book's conclusion, where I share why the phrase *God within us* has new meaning after deconstructing from Christianity. Each chapter will provide you with spiritual nuggets of wisdom, as well as practical action steps that you may find helpful on your healing journey.

No matter where you find yourself at this moment—in church and simply curious, in the midst of spiritual unrest, lost in the spiritual wilderness, or currently traversing the spiritual-but-not-religious path—*Deconstructing* will help you find powerful connection and sacred meaning.

This is your invitation to take the first steps toward a spiritually authentic and empowered life.

While I am inspired by and appreciative of some of what my Christian heritage taught me, I am profoundly grateful that I listened to the still, small voice that called me to look beyond the walls of my faith to seek new ways of understanding humanity and the Divine.

Let us begin the journey together.

And so it is, and blessed be,
Rev Karla

A Word of Caution

Throughout this book, we will be discussing trauma, specifically religious trauma. If you carry trauma from any experience, you may find some of this content unsettling or triggering. While we do not dive into the details of specific kinds of trauma, it is out of an abundance of caution that we offer this here so that you are informed of and prepared for this book's content. Always remember: be gentle with yourself and your healing journey. Seek help if you need it. Take the time and space you need to feel safe.

Preface

Beloved, this is a book about deconstructing your faith.

Trust me on this one.

By the end of chapter 1, this preface will make more sense. From this lived experience that I share here, I came to realize that so often our lived experiences hold wisdom if we are willing to listen and pay attention.

In this book's introduction, I shared what I feel is the process of deconstruction—we *demolish* the structure upon which our faith has been built, *repair* what religion may have done to us, and *restore* our hearts and souls in a way that is authentically who we are.

Here is the story that inspired this wisdom.

Demolish. Repair. Restore.

In 2013, my husband and I began a serious renovation project. Our fifty-plus-year-old home was in dire need of being rescued from its 1970s design, and we were looking forward to bringing our sacred living space into the current decade. Our excitement morphed into exhaustion after discovering the importance of contractor integrity and planning for the unexpected. Months after the original completion date—I vowed to never take part in another remodeling project.

Yet here we were in 2022, and another season of renovations—in the same home, no less—had begun.

You know what they say: "Want to make God laugh? Tell 'Him' your plans." (Throughout the book, I may share another's perspective or belief about God. Quotation marks around *Him* indicate the use of he/him pronouns to describe God do not reflect my belief about God—at least not anymore.)

Admittedly, this project was necessary. The original work from 2013 ended disastrously and incomplete (again contractor integrity, or rather, lack thereof—choose wisely, people!). We decided that we would just live with the inconveniences and chalk it up as experience. However, a house approaching sixty years old will inevitably need some TLC. As groundwater found its way into the subtle cracks in the foundation, we knew it was time to finish what should have been completed nine years earlier.

The water remediation would be a huge undertaking, requiring us to move completely out of the lower level of our home for the team to have access to all areas of the basement. That alone turned into a weeks-long project. Some of the items stored down there hadn't been touched in years. Such is the story of a twenty-eight-plus-year marriage, children, grandchildren, and all our pets. I packed up countless keepsakes for sentimental value or "just in case" I ever needed them again.

As much as this project needed to be done, the timing of it—if I may be so blunt—just sucked. Plopped right in the middle of high moments of loss and sorrow, sprinkled with a few family crises, and some major writing deadlines for upcoming workshops . . . packing, sorting, and moving added a great deal of stress on an already overloaded schedule. Even when I paused for breath and recognized the "goodness" arriving—an opening in the contractors' packed schedule, the finances available to restore our home, and the prospect of finally finishing it in a way that makes it useful and lovable—I still wondered why all these things seemed to be happening at once.

Just Tell God Your Plans

And, boy, did I have plans! I had spent the entire day in a spare bedroom that I lovingly labeled my "war room" because here was where strategy met action. The tables I had set up in there made navigating around the room impossible, but I didn't care. I was the only one using the room, and I needed the tables to visualize the remainder of 2022. To get course material written and some writing completed, I was going to have to be intentional with my time in a way that required a well-thought-out strategy. So, I set out to map every hour of the next few months to determine how much time I needed each day for high-priority and time-sensitive assignments. It was all doable if I stayed focused and kept to this schedule. The sight of all these calendars and Post-it notes would have intimidated anyone looking in on my method of madness. I, however, found it exhilarating as I realized that I had finally found a system that helped me stay organized. Such is life as a creative soul with a need for order and structure.

As I wrapped up this labor of love, confident in my ability to pull this off, I walked out of my office that overlooked our open-style basement and came face-to-face with God's laughter. As the water slowly inched its way out from the corners of the basement, I knew all the planning I had just finished was going right out the window. The water's movement was slow enough that it didn't demand that we stop everything at that moment to move items out of its way. In my mind, however, it might as well have been a tidal wave. Its presence meant that our priorities had just shifted in a significant and profound way.

It happens this way, doesn't it? We have plans for life, then life gets in the way of those plans. The reality is, we often ignore things that need attention, hoping they'll just disappear or, at the very least, become less urgent.

It's not as if we didn't know the water was there. We had seen the swollen wooden trim along the floor's edge for some time. "We'll get to that someday," we'd muse. That someday came blasting toward us in a slow, ominous stream as if to say, "You can't ignore me any longer."

You Can't Ignore Me Any Longer

And so it goes—a period of disruption that will lead to the completion of a home in disrepair for over nine years. A home that desperately needed to address the cracks in its foundation to ensure its viability in the future. A home that needed attention to become a sacred space for all who entered.

We wanted to believe that the cracks weren't there. We wanted to believe that we were okay with substandard work that created chaos in what should have been a safe harbor for our family. We wanted to believe that despite its flaws, we could live like this.

I now laugh along with the Divine as I see the arrogance in my assumptions and the ignorance in my refusal to see the truth.

The truth is cracks in any foundation will always lead to chaos. Brokenness in any system will always lead to someone being harmed. And being in the company of corruption—be they contractors, businesspeople, churchgoers, or politicians—will always allow the corrupt to remain in power.

And those of us stupid enough to believe that things will be okay will lose.

Facing these hard truths, I did the only thing I knew to do.

I dove into *demolishing* what was broken . . .

to *repair* the foundation and ensure its strength . . .

and *restore* the home to make it a safe and sacred space for all.

A demolishing project of this size meant that every space in our home would be affected. Before the project began, I spent hours sorting, rearranging, and packing items in hopes of having some semblance of order. I had saved my beloved war room for last. Part of me didn't want to return to this room where I had spent so much time planning my schedule. I had not had a chance to review the plan since I had created it, let alone implement any component of it.

Eventually, I had no choice but to open the door to set eyes on all the calendars and sticky notes splattered over every inch of it. I wasn't prepared for the emotional rush that threatened to overwhelm me. I had stories to tell and people to reach, but our home needed me as well. A familiar tension began to arise as I considered how often my calling to ministry has collided with my responsibilities as a wife, mother, grandmother, daughter, friend, and so on. This tension between passion and responsibility is a dance we sometimes do for the rest of our lives—that is, if we're lucky. The tension means it's a life that is full of mixed blessings that often collide with something deep inside our souls inviting us to dance with creativity so that something that is uniquely who we are is birthed and offered to the world.

I felt all of that standing over my artwork of calendars and sticky notes. I sensed the need to hold this space a while longer and allow myself to honor the time I had spent creating this visual masterpiece, grieving the time lost as well as the plan that almost was. As I stood there, I became aware that our lived experiences do indeed hold wisdom, and that my war room was the visual representation of a wilderness that is impossible to tame—it can only be experienced.

The wilderness that I now faced with my home reminded me of the spiritual wilderness that I had navigated after leaving church with no calendar, no sticky notes, no road map, and no timeline. Prior to entering the spiritual wilderness, I had for years ignored the suffering in my soul that pointed me to what needed light. I had tried to silence the still, small voice that told me that the God that I was finding in church was being contained in too small a box. I had attempted to contort myself to be what church needed me to be so that I was accepted into the fold of my spiritual community.

Until one day the groundwater surrounding me in church that

I had desperately denied even existed began to seep out into the open. The water from years of dealing with the hypocrisy and spiritual abuse* within the church could no longer be contained, and I could no longer ignore its presence.

I somehow knew that if I heeded this call to step into the spiritual wilderness, I would not be returning to church. With one final look back, I stepped into the spiritual wilderness with only the inner knowing that this was the sacred space into which I was always headed.

We will continue this journey into the spiritual wilderness in chapter 1.

But on that day, standing in this war room and staring at my hard work to bring a rigid structure to my creative process, I realized that the denials in my personal life—that my home needed attention—reflected my journey into the spiritual wilderness, where my soul had beckoned me into a season of discovery and healing. This season that I was entering provided me with the words that I needed to offer to those who find themselves standing alone in that spiritual wilderness. Words that I hadn't realized so accurately reflected the journey into and through it.

Beloved: demolish, repair, restore. *Demolish* the structure, *repair* the harm, *restore* the heart and soul. That is the only guidance needed for your time in the spiritual wilderness and on your deconstructing journey.

It doesn't require a war room.

It requires trust, patience, and a commitment to stay here if needed to complete the work. Hastily done work will ensure the water will return to compromise the foundation, and the pattern of denial, frustration, and surrender is repeated. The time in the spiritual wilderness may be some of the most challenging work that you will do, but it will be the most rewarding.

Now that you understand what inspired my discovering how the wisdom of demolishing, repairing, and restoring shaped my deconstructing journey, you will find at the end of each chapter a resource box where I offer practical and tangible ways for you to take actions on the teachings I offer.

Or not. There is no judgment on the progress or decisions you make along the way. Deconstructing is as personal a journey as any other sacred passage in our lives.

Are You Ready, Beloved?

Are you ready to learn about what it means to deconstruct? To spend time in the spiritual wilderness? To reclaim your spirituality and live a spiritually empowered life?

Are you ready to demolish, repair, and restore?

Then come. Let us learn what it means to leave the certainty of your religious heritage and find your spiritual truth on your deconstructing journey.

Healing, wisdom, and peace await.

The Spiritual Wilderness

When the Faith of Our Heritage
No Longer Makes Sense

Unless you have walked through it and have come out on the other side, you'll never understand. And when you're in the middle of it, there can never be enough reassurance that you are gonna be okay.

I found this in my journal, written sometime after my ordination in 2017. Looking back, I realize that this is the most accurate description of the period after I began my deconstruction journey to heal from religious trauma and release my indoctrinated beliefs from modern evangelical Christianity. I also realize it reveals little about my experience that would be helpful to someone who finds themselves in a similar place.

To get to that moment in 2017 when I wrote that in my journal, we need to return to where it all began. From there, we can build a bridge from the little girl growing up Southern Baptist to the woman who in her fifties began a yearslong journey to untangle herself from her religious heritage.

Ever Since I Was a Little Girl, I Loved Jesus

I have many memories of church on Sunday morning and Sunday evening, and Wednesday Bible study. My grandmother, a passionate and staunch Southern Baptist, instilled in me a commitment to Christianity as the keeper of my faith and the guidepost for my morality.

Most summers centered around spending time at my grandmother's home in Kentucky. My mother, a single mom who often worked two jobs to keep a roof over our heads, relied on the care of grandparents for summer breaks because childcare was simply not in the budget. I didn't mind. When you're poor, any trip beyond your small town feels like a vacation. Besides, I adored my grandmother. I loved to watch her craft her floral arrangements, the smell of her coffee brewing in the wee hours, and the sight of her well-worn Bible that usually was within arm's reach from wherever she was seated.

I often wonder how different her life would have been if she had ever lived beyond the dogma of her religion—the one that told her that she could never be a pastor. She damn sure would have been better than any of her kinfolk who were pastors—all men—because I knew no one with a hotter fire in her belly for God or a mightier voice that bellowed her passion across the room.

Yes, my deeply religious and devoted grandmother was the foundation of my religious indoctrination. She taught me early that heavenly rewards awaited the faithful and to not question the mysteries of God. Those bookends—heavenly reward and silent submission—are chasms apart. Much later in life, I would come to understand that these bookends of the promises of heaven and earthly obedience were intentional, carefully designed to encapsulate the entirety of the human experience. In other words, put God first in all facets of your life, and do not look to the world for answers. For therein lies the blessings of salvation for the obedient.

And obedient I was. I picked up this message earnestly even as a young child. This is why I almost never hesitated to miss an opportunity to be in church. If my grandmother's car was headed to church, I was more than likely in it. Oftentimes, I may have been the only grandchild going. The others often opted to take advantage of a quiet home to sleep in or catch up on Sunday cartoons.

Vacation Bible school was not optional, however. And as usual, I didn't mind, of course, because this is where I soaked in each day's lesson and sang all the traditional songs at the top of my lungs, such as "Jesus Loves Me" and "This Little Light of Mine."

My Southern Baptist upbringing differs from that of other children my age. As much as I loved children's Sunday school and vacation Bible school, what I most enjoyed was sitting in worship with my grandmother. There I would sit motionless, listening to the preachers, captivated by their passion and their unending flow of words that seemed to come right down from heaven. I believed with my whole heart the words of parishioners who said that the pastors were true "men of God," because only men of God could preach like that. So deep was my desire to be in the presence of adults studying "the Word" that I often accompanied her to adult Bible study instead of attending children's Sunday school.

This was life in a small town in Kentucky in the '60s. A time when more people went to church than not. Even school activities and public events were planned around the church calendar.

Much has changed since then.

The Fear of God and Tent Revivals

The arrival of the touring ministers who held the tent revivals signaled that summer would soon be ending. Summer tent revivals were deeply ingrained in the Southern Baptist tradition. My grandmother never missed a night of these weeklong events, and I went right along with her, often not returning until well past 10:00 p.m. The name itself, *tent revival*, reflects the intention of these high-energy and passionate events—a time to revive your soul and recommit your faith. The most energetic and emotionally charged preachers were chosen to lead these revivals, often touring throughout the summer and speaking to packed tents that were usually standing room only each and every night.

I was completely mesmerized by the cinematic performance of the preacher while he preached the message that Jesus would return, we would be raptured to heaven, and those who didn't believe would suffer eternal damnation in hell. In my preadolescent mind, I often found myself overwhelmed and many times downright terrified by what was being preached. Yet I was transfixed on the larger-than-life preacher prancing about onstage, screaming one minute to reflect the vengeance and anger of a jealous God, then whispering the next with tears running down his face to assure us that it's only out of love that God is vengeful and angry toward us. When you experience this paradox of love displayed as anger, you can see why this type of religious indoctrination is the catalyst for religious trauma that manifests later in life for those exposed to it in childhood.

This is something I will talk about throughout this book.

Some of those sermons impacted me so greatly that I can recall every detail of the revival's evening, sitting in that tent with my grandmother. The lack of a breeze on those hot Kentucky summer nights made for a sweltering experience that would drench me in sweat from head to toe. No one seemed to mind, evidenced by the occasional praises of "Hallelujah!" and "Amen!" from those standing-room-only crowds. The sweat poured from the preacher's face, but he never wavered in his commitment to deliver a powerful sermon, sometimes preaching for hours at a time. No one dared leave early—that was as taboo as showing up on Sunday with an uncovered tattoo. I didn't mind the long nights. Even for me, a young girl of about ten years old, it seemed as if time stood still. I soaked in every word as if my life depended on it.

In some ways, my life *did* depend upon it. I just didn't know it at the time. Years later, I would discover that the very thing that I was searching for inside church would be that which would beckon me to turn away from the preachers' sermons and listen to that still, small voice inside of me. That still, small voice was inviting me to step away from the structure of my religious heritage and seek a new understanding of faith, spirituality, Jesus, and God.

Leaving Church and Entering the Spiritual Wilderness

The bridge from my childhood to becoming unchurched is a long one, and by the end of this book, you will understand more about that journey. What is important now, Beloved, is for you to be assured that if my story resonates with you because it sounds familiar, then rest assured that things do get better and your spiritual path becomes clearer as time goes on.

Depending on where you are on your spiritual journey, your past may seem irreconcilable with your beliefs now. You may not recognize yourself in your own story. Those of us who grow beyond our beliefs and narratives that others forced upon us rarely do. But if you trust that where you are right now will point you to your spiritual truth, healing and clarity will come.

I had spent close to fifty years beholden to this religion that began in those church pews and tent revivals in the hills of Kentucky. Little did I know the religion that said I, as a woman, could never preach in their churches would be an integral part of my life story that later inspired me to ministry. The paradox of my religious indoctrination—one that rejects a woman's right to be an ordained minister—as being the birthplace of my call to ministry is not lost on me. It is in these life experiences, the ones that at one time felt true and safe that—if you're willing to sit still and listen—self-awareness will come that can provide the building blocks for the rest of your spiritual journey.

To get there—to that space of self-awareness—you must first leave the comfort of the known and step into the unknown.

It does happen. There is a reconciliation that occurs, but it takes time, Beloved. And to get to that place where your authentic self is waiting, you will enter a season in what I call the *spiritual wilderness*.

What Is the Spiritual Wilderness?

The spiritual wilderness often begins when you have had a crisis of faith or a falling away from a belief system that no longer serves your highest good. It is when something has shifted inside you in such a palpable way that you simply cannot ignore it beckoning you to its edges and inviting you to dive into its murky yet calm waters of unlearning and unpacking beliefs and ideologies that no longer resonate with who you are becoming.

It's an invitation to listen to that still, small voice deep inside you that you most likely have been rejecting as authentic for a period of time—sometimes a lifetime.

The spiritual wilderness can be a time when you feel alone and vulnerable with no clear path to navigate your time in it, no time frame for how long it will last, no one to tell you what to expect next, and no idea of the outcome. I'm intentionally vague about this description because it's as unique for each person as our fingerprints—no two experiences within the spiritual wilderness are the same.

The spiritual wilderness is not only a place where your long-held beliefs are challenged but also where you confront who you are as a human being. It's where words and their meanings begin to fall away, and in their place, questions arise:

- How can so many other religions exist and only one be right?
- How can I know what to believe is true in the Bible when the Bible has been translated and edited so many times?
- Does hell really exist?
- Who—or even what—is God?
- Is my understanding of heaven true?
- Who am I if I'm not what I was taught to believe about who I was?
- Do I really want to know the answers to these questions, or do I just want to fall back asleep and "fake it in the pews"?

These and so many more questions may have arisen as you consider exploring the spiritual wilderness for yourself. Any one of these questions can rattle your soul and shake the ground upon which you are standing. *After all, do you truly want to come face-to-face with a mirror that is challenging everything you thought you knew about the mysteries of the Divine?*

How Did I Get Here?

Although the experience differs greatly for everyone, there are some similarities in how we all arrived in the spiritual wilderness. For some, a crisis of faith was prompted by an abrupt—and often tragic—life event. The death of a loved one, a betrayal, or a loss of control over your finances that jeopardizes your well-being are just a few examples. It is during these times when we turn to our spiritual community and our faith, and for whatever reason, they failed us miserably. One of my spiritual-care clients shared that after the death of his father, his home church did little to comfort his grief. Instead, they dismissed his sorrow and reminded him that his father was now in heaven and he should be happy. He wasn't happy, and he couldn't envision a time when he could be. Because of their hyperfocus on salvation, they simply lacked the empathy and awareness to hold the space this person needed to grieve his father. These types of indoctrinated beliefs can often detach people from dealing with the suffering in the world, ill equipping the indoctrinated to show up with compassion. For my client, his church's inability to be there for him opened his eyes to how little his church cared about the well-being of its members, and he began to look deeply at his own beliefs, their value for his life, and how little they helped elevate the human condition. Eventually, he left that church and found community in another one after he deconstructed from the indoctrinated beliefs that no longer served his highest good.

It doesn't have to be a tragic occurrence that beckons you toward the spiritual wilderness. It can be something as simple as trying to explain your understanding of God to an inquisitive child whose authentic curiosity challenges your indoctrinated beliefs. You may have been taught that "our ways are not God's ways" or that "we've reached the end of our limited human understanding of the Divine," code for "you should stop asking further questions or you will be seen as being weak in faith." But a child who has not been indoctrinated this way simply wants to understand why her prayers were not answered and her best friend is still moving away.

Our own questions, doubts, or even fears oftentimes crash into our beliefs when we experience them through the eyes of another who simply cannot understand why we believe the way we do.

Or perhaps that someone is you.

It was for me.

I can now see that I was drifting away from a religious indoctrination that not only didn't serve my highest good but also demanded an allegiance to an outdated theology that condemned large swaths of humanity. My pushing on the outer edges of those indoctrinated beliefs created a tension inside me that I simply could no longer ignore.

Each of us has entered the spiritual wilderness from a different life experience, and I am sure you have as well. Whether you came to the spiritual wilderness through an abrupt life change or through a subtle shift from deep inside you, the thought of navigating your spirituality outside the comfort of your spiritual community can be unsettling.

The Paradox of the Spiritual Wilderness
When Deconstructing from Your Faith

The paradox of the spiritual wilderness arrived immediately for me after I left the church. I found myself in a surreal space of peace for having finally left a toxic church environment yet anxiety for where I was going.

I would often find myself pondering what I was experiencing.

How can something so undefinable and so lonely be understood and appreciated by the people who find themselves there? Why would someone be willing to navigate it after hearing of others' experiences with it? Who will I be once I come out the other side of it?

Whether you are standing on the edges of this spiritual wilderness, fearful of entering it, or whether you are deep in the sacred abyss of its mystery, I hope my story about my time in the spiritual wilderness will give you the assurance that this paradox you may be experiencing is exactly what you need.

It is important to remember that my life's journey of navigating through Christianity and then ultimately deconstructing from it and leaving the church forever is just that—my healing journey. Since I have memories of attending adult Bible study when I was six years old, that means that this journey spans well over fifty years. Your journey will look much different from mine and the millions of others who are also on this deconstruction journey. The most important thing to remember is that wherever you are in the spiritual wilderness—afraid to enter or are deep within it—your individual experience may leave you with an entirely different definition of what it is and how it has impacted you emotionally and spiritually.

Read these words through the filter of this lens so that my experience does not become yet another dogma or doctrine you must follow and therefore hinder your individual experience.

It's also important to emphasize here that deconstruction arrives, manifests, and ends in many forms. As I look back, I now see that it was clear that my deconstructing journey had begun long before I had made the decision to leave the church. The starting point of deconstructing is different for each of us, and who you are once you have experienced it will most certainly be different. Focusing on the logistics of when, how, and how long may cause you to miss the point.

And the point?

Heal what is broken, Beloved, by demolishing, repairing, and restoring so that you too can reclaim your spirituality and live a spiritually empowered life.

The Spiritual Wilderness Is the
Proverbial Dark Night of the Soul

When first learning about the spiritual wilderness, you may find it helpful to compare it to a spiritual concept that is prevalent in many Christian teachings—the concept of the dark night of the soul.* I first discovered this concept in the writing of Saint John of the Cross called *La Noche Oscura del Alma*, translated into English as *Dark Night of the Soul*.[1] Saint John of the Cross, a sixteenth-century Catholic friar and practitioner of mysticism and asceticism,* endured horrific abuse during his imprisonment by his own Carmelite brothers, who opposed his reform efforts within the order. He was imprisoned in a tiny cell where he experienced regular beatings and inhumane living conditions. He would eventually escape his captors, but his imprisonment significantly influenced his mystical and spiritual insights, which eventually became his work *Dark Night of the Soul* after his escape.

Although I was familiar with the phrase *dark night of the soul*, I had never heard of Saint John of the Cross prior to discovering his writings. Evangelical Christianity pays little mind to mystics and saints in the Roman Catholic Church like Saint John of the Cross. I was immediately pulled into his writings. They felt eerily familiar even though they had been written centuries earlier in another part of the world from a man whose lived experience looked nothing like my own.

As I sat reading *Dark Night of the Soul*, I couldn't help but wonder what had compelled him to write words that echoed up to today with such resonance. Words such as "No other light, no other guide than the one burning in my heart."

To me, those words revealed a profound crisis of faith for Saint John of the Cross. Within his crisis of faith, I found comfort and affirmation. He was someone who had dedicated his life to the

Christian faith; thus, I too had permission to acknowledge and perhaps even welcome the anguish, doubt, and fear permeating my mind and soul.

One of the many paradoxes of the spiritual wilderness is revealed here. In his dark night of the soul, a Carmelite monk from the sixteenth century wrote of his anguish and desperation to find and experience a God that he believed only revealed "Himself" through his Christian faith. The words of Saint John of the Cross found their way to a woman sitting on her couch in Indiana. With every word she read, that Christian faith to which Saint John of the Cross was so beholden hundreds of years ago began to loosen its grip on her. So much so that she would very soon realize that her dark night of the soul was pointing her away from her religious heritage.

And out of the church forever.

What Is Your Dark Night of the Soul?

Whatever its origins—an emotional crisis, a crisis of faith, tragedy, sorrow, or even stress and anxiety—the concept of the dark night of the soul offers peace and comfort to those who felt isolated and alone, certain that they were the only one who has ever felt this alone, with no answers and no path forward.

The truth is the dark night of the soul is a more common human experience than many of us ever understood. My evangelical Christian heritage had taught me early on that "big feelings" were bad and questioning your faith was even worse. Discovering that my crisis of faith was not only normal but that it also was sacred provided me the assurance I needed to trust that my doubts and questions would point me to a deeper spirituality than I had ever discovered in my evangelical roots.

That journey from leaving the church to entering the spiritual wilderness and finding comfort within my dark night of the soul would be foundational for my healing the broken parts of me caused by toxic religious and familial experiences that I had endured throughout my life. It is here that I untangled myself from harmful narratives that had been placed upon me about who I was and the ways I was supposed to show up in the world. In those spaces where those harmful narratives used to live inside of me now exists my true authentic self, who is no longer beholden to religious ideologies who saw me as less than simply because of my gender.

That journey was work—hard work. But every step, every tear, every minute of sitting without answers and wondering if I would ever receive it was worth it.

Beloved, what of you? What is your dark night of the soul? Where is your spiritual wilderness taking you? Do not worry if you don't have answers to these questions. Not having the answers simply means you have more time in this sacred season of deconstructing from harmful narratives to discover what lies deep within you.

Each of us walks this spiritual wilderness path differently. Our dark-night-of-the-soul experiences are uniquely ours as well. For Saint John of the Cross, the phrase *dark night of the soul* meant that the journey of the soul to Divine union with God is filled with moments of spiritual crises and feelings of abandonment. It meant that the inner struggle where one feels most distant from God is the place where—if you trust that our darkness can point us to wisdom and clarity—you will find union with this Divine mystery.

For me, I discovered that the dark night of a faith crisis is more common than we are led to believe.

It meant these dark nights often led to feelings of abandonment and confusion.

It meant the dark night of the soul is where the most profound healing occurs and where the most valuable intuitive wisdom arrives.

Here is where authentic healing begins, Beloved.

The dark night of the soul.

A phrase penned by sixteenth-century mystic Saint John of the Cross, who was desperate to find Divine union when all he felt was spiritual dryness, desolation, and abandonment.

In *Dark Night of the Soul*, he wrote:

> Beloved, you pray, please remind me again and again that I am nothing. Strip me of the consolations of my complacent spirituality. Plunge me into the darkness where I cannot rely on many of my old tricks for maintaining my separation. Let me give up on trying to convince myself that my own spiritual deeds are bound to be pleasing to you.[2]

The phrase *dark night of the soul* echoes up to us today as an invitation to rethink what a crisis of faith is signaling to us. Its wisdom is found in many of the world's spiritual and religious traditions.

→ The idea of facing inner darkness to emerge into the light can be seen in concepts like the Buddhist notion of *dukkha* (suffering) leading to enlightenment.

→ Modern spiritual teachers, such as Eckhart Tolle, Deepak Chopra, and Thomas Moore, have drawn upon the concept to describe moments of profound existential* crisis that lead to spiritual awakening.

→ Some modern psychotherapists and counselors recognize the value of the dark night in personal transformation. Religious inference is stripped away from this concept; however, they see the value of facing and moving through personal darkness.

How we arrive at our dark night of the soul is irrelevant. Our spiritual journeys are as vast as the world religions and Christian denominational theologies that may have influenced us. No one path is the one true path, and no path is more important or sacred than another.

cont'd

Embracing our dark night connects us to those who have come before us and have experienced the same. Each of us builds collectively upon another's experience, moving us ever so slightly closer to the ultimate truth about who or what God is and our connection to the Holy.

After reading *Dark Night of the Soul,* I wrote this:

"Bright flows the river of God. When there is nothing else to reach for . . . when God is all you have . . . then look for God right where you are." There is immense wisdom in his [Saint John of the Cross's] words, for most of us—the action would be impossible—the pain just too deep. Yet here we stand, with history providing us the way of the mystics. It is up to us to receive it or reject it. Saint John of the Cross offers no judgment on our decision. His poetry will be here for another day and another season in our lives when we may be ready to fully embrace the path that comes from living with faith. For within the dark night of the soul, just as in the daylight, is God.

Once we accept that the dark night of the soul could be one of our most powerful spiritual transformations, we are ready. It is time to step into the healing and wisdom awaiting you in the spiritual wilderness.

The Spiritual Unrest in Your Life's Experiences: The Spiritual Breadcrumbs

I am often asked if there was a specific incident or situation that prompted me to leave the church, embrace my dark night of the soul, and enter the spiritual wilderness. For some people, it can be an isolated incident, but more than likely, it was a lifetime of events. I call them *spiritual breadcrumbs*: those things that seemed inconsequential when they happened yet become aha moments when you reflect on your spiritual journey. When reviewed in their entirety as moments in your spiritual life, you finally realize you can no longer ignore how all those spiritual breadcrumbs impacted you.

I have many spiritual breadcrumbs that I'll share throughout this book. At the time they happened, they were often concerning, even downright painful. Some of them were just moments of awareness that should have indicated that I was willing to explore spirituality outside of my religious heritage.

As an example, I was fascinated by psychic mediums. I would covertly watch nationally renowned medium John Edward's television show *Crossing Over* but would quickly change the channel if someone entered the room. I also began reading books by Bishop John Shelby Spong. Bishop Spong's teachings would eventually become a spiritual lifeline for me. Back then, however, I was certainly not leaving his book *Why Christianity Must Change or Die* lying around on my coffee table!

Having navigated the spiritual wilderness and now on a spiritual-but-not-religious path, I have been able to heal from the harm that I had experienced inside the church. It was worth it so that I could reclaim my spirituality and live a life that is more authentic and empowering. You too will find this as you take this journey through the spiritual wilderness.

For me, it would take many years of work on my religious trauma and my spiritual truth to finally say that I was living a spiritually empowered life (we will expand on this in chapter 9). In 2011, when I was deeply immersed in an evangelical/Pentecostal church, I had never even heard phrases like *reclaiming your spirituality* or *deconstructing your faith*.

All I knew at that time was that I could no longer ignore the reality that was bubbling up inside me—I was leaving the church. I hadn't told anyone other than my husband, who was equally frustrated and unconditionally supportive of my growing desire to leave the church. After a series of events where I had been manipulated by church leaders and even told that I had a spirit of offense* for challenging some troubling behavior by those leaders, I knew that my time had come to leave.

I just didn't know what life would look like after leaving. The church had been my beacon for my entire life. It was my spiritual community, my religious identity, and where relationships were oftentimes closer and more sacred than with my family. All I knew was that wherever I was going had to be better than the pain I was experiencing trying to contort myself to fit a dogma that I no longer believed. A dogma that had become so weaponized and conditional that it no longer looked anything like the teachings of Jesus. A dogma that I had witnessed time and again be used to judge, condemn, and persecute those who did not look like, love like, or believe like those inside the church.

This was not heaven on earth, as the church liked to market itself.

This was hell.

And so, on that day years ago, as I made my way to the exit, I knew I was stepping out of this church for the final time. What I didn't expect was that my relief was quickly met with guilt, my peace was met with sorrow, and the silence I craved was met with confusion.

Why? Because this was a place I had never been—unchurched. Without a road map, friends, or a spiritual compass to tell me what was next, I took my first steps into the unknown. I just didn't know at the time that this unknown had a name—the spiritual wilderness.

Now What? Learn It for Yourself

The most terrifying moments after leaving the church came when I realized that no one would—or even could—answer the question, "Now what?" for me. I was desperately looking for some kind of structure or something in this wilderness that was familiar to the corporate worship of my religious heritage. In other words, I was looking for the rule book that would define God and explain what I was to expect.

This is a fragile and precarious time for a person whose spirituality has been filtered through someone else's definition of God. With that gone, there is only you—and God.

Well, you are here.

But where is God?

Day after day, nothing came. There were times I trusted this spiritual wilderness, and there were many more when I doubted myself to the point of considering returning to the church because of the void I felt threatened to overtake what I believed to be my calling.

Some do return. When they speak of their spiritual wilderness, they admit that doubt compelled them to return, opting instead to fake it in the pews—pretending to believe to belong. Sound familiar? Sadly, this is all too common. Remembering my own doubts and feelings of loneliness, I now fully understand.

For many of us, the calling of the spiritual wilderness was too strong, and we chose to stay in the unknown. For me, that meant no longer looking for a rule book to fall back on. Instead, I trusted and waited.

My journey took me through intense and life-changing soul work that redefined my relationships and gave me the tools to unpack and begin healing my personal and religious trauma. Being accountable led me to the space that I had been longing for my entire life.

The space where God lives in humanity, not in one religion's ideology.

Looking back on my time in the spiritual wilderness, I also realize that I was asking the wrong question.

"Now what?" is unanswerable.

It's undefinable.

It's expectation-less.

It's also arrogant because it assumes answers will come from somewhere out there when, all along, they're waiting to be discovered within.

For years, there has been speculation that the iconic movie *The Wizard of Oz* carried themes of spirituality hidden inside its mythical tale. Perhaps it does, because each time I arrive at this point in my story, I see the image of Glinda the Good Witch in my mind's eye. Dorothy was longing to go home after searching far and wide in a fantastical adventure that included demonic flying monkeys and a battle with the most powerful of all beings whom people fearfully revered (once again the paradox of loving a vengeful and angry God).

Leaning in to capture her undivided attention, in the gentlest and most loving of voices, Glinda assures Dorothy, "You've always had the power . . ." Glinda explains to a confused and perplexed Dorothy that Dorothy would not have believed in this power because "she had to learn it for herself."

"Learn it for yourself" was exactly what a mentor, whose ancestral heritage was deep in the shamanic traditions of the People (whom we know as Native Americans), had said to me when I sought her wisdom after entering the spiritual wilderness. Alone, bitter, and extremely angry at Christianity, she offered me this: "Karla, you will navigate this vast spiritual void, and you will not only come out on the other side of it healed and whole. You will look back on the path that you have walked, wave to others, and say, 'Here—this way.' But first, you must *learn it for yourself*. Trust this season. After a lifetime of thinking you know everything about God, the not-knowing is exactly what you need."

Exactly what I need?! How could something so unsettling and foreign be exactly what I needed? But I trusted her wisdom because the way I saw my choice was to either give up entirely on my spiritual journey or to return to the church, fake it in the pews, and spend the rest of my life being spoon-fed from the pulpit the same toxic beliefs that had harmed me for decades.

I wasn't ready to give up, and I certainly wasn't returning to the church. This is when I realized that even though I didn't know where I was going or how long it would take me to discover it, I was going to learn it for myself by trusting this new journey. Taking a deep breath, I set my resolve to finish what had begun years earlier when, as a little girl, I tried to understand why my church didn't think I could be a minister. I dove into the spiritual wilderness and began my journey to *demolish* the structure upon which my faith had been built, *repair* the harm religion had done to me, and *restore* my heart and soul so that I could live a spiritually empowered life.

And finally . . .

Understanding that the spiritual wilderness is the work of the soul—the kind of work that invites you to hold up a mirror to your authentic self so that you can truly understand the person who is staring back at you. That person is here in this moment in time for a reason. And your time in the spiritual wilderness is an invitation to dive in, trust the process, and discover what needs to be healed, what needs light, and what needs to be released.

Make no mistake about it. This was hard work. Though it was hard, I don't regret it. Not for one second. Once I understood that learning it for myself did not mean that I had to do it alone, I began to find others on a similar journey. Others who were ahead on the path were turning toward me, waving their hands, and saying, "Here—this way."

That is the main difference between time in the spiritual wilderness and being spoon-fed from the pulpit—the latter says, "Believe this"; the former invites you to discover it on your own.

Your time in the spiritual wilderness isn't about who you will be once your time there is over. This is the very you that is waiting to be discovered once you've navigated the wilderness. The spiritual wilderness doesn't mandate an allegiance to a belief system or a religion. It also doesn't say that you must steer clear of them. Each person's journey is different. I am comfortable in my spiritual skin as an unchurched, nonconforming Christian who walks the spiritual-but-not-religious path (we'll return to this in chapter 9).

I vow to remain curious on this path, and I also know that by staying curious, my path and how I define myself may change.

When I first entered the wilderness as an angry, bitter Christian
who wanted to expose the harm church does, I never would have
imagined that I could heal to the point where I could ever reconcile with my Christian heritage. But I have, and I'm so grateful
that I did the work to arrive here.

I just had to learn it for myself.

One of the most poignant and healing moments in my journey
through the spiritual wilderness is this: God is not hiding inside
any one religion. God is in the everyday moments of our lives.
God is in our lived experiences.

God is.

Beloved,

Demolish. Repair. Restore.

*I offer this chapter to assure you that your
deconstructing journey most likely will include time in the
spiritual wilderness, where you may also discover a season
where you will come face-to-face with your own dark
night of the soul. I hope what I shared here encourages
you to trust this journey and be open to accepting that
what arrives is exactly what you need.*

*The time in the spiritual wilderness is the season
of demolition—an invitation to deconstruct from
conditioned beliefs so they no longer influence or harm
you as you continue this healing journey. Making a
commitment to do the work of breaking down the rigid
structures upon which your faith was built frees you from
dogmatic beliefs that restrict how you view the world and
your place in it.*

*This is the transformative nature of deconstructing, and
your time demolishing is a crucial step toward personal
and spiritual growth.*

Here are some action steps that may help guide you on your journey:

→ *Read. I cannot emphasize this enough. We often are taught only one scriptural interpretation of the Bible and have never been exposed to other wisdom keepers and teachers. See my suggested readings at the end of the book.*

→ *Research other ways to practice prayer and meditation. Prayer was often weaponized in some church traditions to remind us that we are sinners, broken, and that we need to ask God for forgiveness. When we are ready to untangle from that kind of prayer, we can discover new meaning in prayer by exploring how other traditions pray. Consider Christian centering prayer or contemplative exercises. These recommendations also appear at the end of this book.*

→ *Keep a spiritual wilderness journal. If journaling doesn't feel right, consider a log on your iPad or phone, or an audio recording of your thoughts and memories. It isn't uncommon for memories to arise that you have forgotten about from years ago—memories that are spiritual breadcrumbs that point you to the places where you were deconstructing. This is a good opportunity to process emotions surrounding your beliefs, your spiritual community, and the like.*

→ *Begin to consider who belongs in your inner circle. It is important to have people whom you can trust and who know how to hold the space and allow you to share your experiences. This doesn't have to be someone physically close. Virtual opportunities abound for discovering connection.*

→ *If a spiritual counselor or therapist is an option for you, consider seeking their help. It isn't uncommon to have* *strong emotions around deconstructing, and they are experienced in helping people with untangling from these emotions. Seek counselors and therapists who are trauma-informed.* This is particularly important if you have experienced abuse or trauma in other aspects of your life.*

→ *Create a timeline journal. This is a powerful exercise to see how you have changed over time. It can also help you see how your own spiritual breadcrumbs were pointing you to your deconstructing. Throughout this book, I will suggest other timelines that you can create to bring clarity to this healing journey.*

Remember: be gentle with yourself and take your time. This work is hard yet worth it—challenging yet healing—painful yet sacred.

The future you is worth it.

Keep going.

Emotional Fallout

Is Deconstructing a Huge Mistake?

Here's the chapter where I explain why I owe a debt of gratitude to C. S. Lewis, Bishop John Shelby Spong, and, yes, King Henry VIII.

It will soon make sense—trust me, Beloved.

Deconstructing your faith: this is a relatively new way to define the process of rethinking your faith. I used to call it *the great spiritual untangling from your religious indoctrination to find your authentic spiritual self*, which is a great deal wordier than merely saying *deconstructing your faith*.

The term *deconstruction* wasn't known to me until I began sharing my story on social media and met other creators who were doing the same. Someone labeled the experience of rethinking your faith as deconstructing from it, and it has stuck.

Labeling our individual experiences of reexamining our religious heritage as deconstructing our faith doesn't mean that our experiences mirror one another's or that our deconstruction happens overnight. Our deconstructing journeys are often more different from how they are alike in experience and in their outcomes.

Deconstruction can happen quickly for some, but for many of us, it takes years. If hearing that it could take years alarms you, it shouldn't. Actively deconstructing from religion and being committed to peeling back every single layer of indoctrinated religious beliefs ensures you've completely examined every aspect of your beliefs and how those beliefs have influenced how you see the world.

Just as it does when you heal from a painful experience in your life, deconstructing from your religious heritage takes time. Rest assured the work is worth it. Peace of mind and a healed heart can be found in those moments between your first steps into the spiritual wilderness of deconstruction and those final steps when you emerge from this wilderness with the clarity and sacred wisdom for which you have been searching.

Let's begin this discussion by exploring what deconstruction is and why your religious heritage, family values, education, and even your demographics all play an important part in what your deconstruction journey will look like.

Defining Deconstruction

At the beginning of this chapter, I offered my definition of deconstruction—*the great spiritual untangling from your religious indoctrination to find your authentic spiritual self*. Another person who has deconstructed may offer an entirely different definition that would more accurately describe their experience.

After years of living with the spiritual road map that religion provided, this definition may feel unsettling to you, as it did to me at first. I remember my own fear as I stepped away from the comfort of organized religion and began searching for a new road map that would help guide me to where I was going. The problem was I didn't know where to find it or even who to ask for directions. Church provided a structure that told me when to be in community, how to worship, and what to believe.

Its absence left me feeling vulnerable and spiritually wobbly. So wobbly were some of those moments that, as I shared earlier, I even considered returning to the church to fake it in the pews. It isn't uncommon for people who *thought* they wanted to deconstruct to find themselves back in church, because spirituality without the structure of organized religion feels too foreign.

Church was not only my community, it was my identity. My entire life had been wrapped up in my desire to be labeled a good Christian, which meant I tithed, sought to obey the teachings of the church, and volunteered an inordinate amount of time to the operations within the church.

Although I was typically at the church several times each week and often overwhelmed by the ever-increasing requests for my time, finding myself free from those responsibilities did not bring me feelings of relief as one might imagine. For the first time in my life, I was on the outside looking in at the religion of my heritage. Where text messages once flooded my phone daily from fellow church members, now there was only silence. Where piles of papers that held the details for the upcoming church event used to clutter our dining table, now there was empty space, the papers neatly boxed away and returned to the church for the next volunteer team to take over. Where details flooded my calendar with Bible studies, leadership meetings, ministry training sessions, coffee with fellow church members, and accountability sessions with church leaders, now there was a blank.

I recall many days sitting on my front porch sobbing because of this loneliness. My spiritual community was everything to me. Never had I considered what life would be if I weren't an obedient, submissive, hardworking, tithe-giving Christian.

But now there was no denying that the unthinkable had indeed happened.

I was now unchurched without the tools to process how I ended up here and what would happen next.

The Decision to Leave: The Spiritual Breadcrumbs

I mentioned in chapter 1 that we often have spiritual breadcrumbs, subtle occurrences that may have seemed insignificant at the time but in hindsight become markers on our spiritual paths. When considered collectively, it becomes undeniable how profoundly these spiritual breadcrumbs have shaped and influenced us.

My spiritual breadcrumbs began as early as nine years old, when I first became aware of inconsistencies in church teachings about my ability to be all that God made me to be, except I couldn't be a minister, because apparently, I misheard that—girls couldn't be ministers. Those breadcrumbs kept dropping as I became keenly aware that my questions related to those inconsistencies were not welcome, and I risked losing my label as a good Christian if I persisted.

Through the twists and turns of my life's journey, those crumbs kept dropping, like when two men showed up at our house one evening, informing my mother that as registered Southern Baptists who lived near their church, it was time for me to be baptized. This occurred when I was about twelve years old. My mother worked the night shift, and regular church attendance was not an option. We, of course, always made it to church for the two Sundays that are must-attends in Southern Baptists' lives—Easter and Christmas. The doctrine of "once saved, always saved"—a tenet of the Baptist faith—offered comfort to the non-regular-attending adults that their salvation was not contingent upon regular church attendance.

But what of me?

Well, up until my twelfth birthday, I was covered under the Southern Baptist belief that if I had died before I was capable of "moral action," then I was bound for heaven. I wasn't really comforted by those teachings. Like most children, I didn't want to ponder my own death, even if it meant I'd be in heaven with Jesus. I wanted to feel safe and secure in my own surroundings, which for me turned out to be elusive. That is the reality of a childhood with a single mother who worked at night, a slew of babysitters coming to sleep over while she worked, and an absent father who prioritized his latest girlfriend and golf over spending time with his children.

I didn't want to be with Jesus. I just wanted to feel safe and loved in my home.

Yet here I was, sitting on my couch and facing two strangers who were now requesting that my mother leave the room so they could speak to me about my salvation. That was my only cue that I had entered the age where my salvation was no longer guaranteed and it had become my responsibility. My mother, fully indoctrinated into the Southern Baptist religious patriarchy,* didn't bat an eye. Without saying a word or even looking my way to see if I was okay with this situation, she quickly exited the room. I was left alone with these two men.

How had this happened? It was just a typical weeknight, the quiet hours that I dreaded as evening fell, and the clock ticked closer to the time my mother would leave for work. The babysitter of the night hadn't arrived, and my only solace was to be *The Carol Burnett Show* until it was my bedtime. Tim Conway made me giggle. Even thinking about it as I write brings a smile to my face.

But *The Carol Burnett Show* was the furthest thing from my mind as the two men joined me on the couch, one on each side of me. Not intimidating at all for a young girl to be surrounded by men who smelled of mothballs and Old Spice. They were dressed in dated topcoats and hats as if they had just walked out of an episode of *Mad Men* on their way to their corporate office. It never occurred to me then that not removing their coats and hats signaled their expectation that this would be a quick exchange.

It was, indeed a quick exchange, and as I replay that moment in my mind, seeing it through the eyes of my age now, how dare they.

How dare they assume that it was within their right to enter a home—on a school night, no less—to speak privately to an unaccompanied minor. Even worse, how dare they instigate that situation by requesting the mother leave the room?

How dare they move so close to a child that her personal space was violated, to ensure the expediency of their assignment?

How dare they willingly perpetuate a religious patriarchy that relied on the silent submission to ensure its perpetuity?

I didn't think of any of this in the moment. I was just a young kid, not even a teenager. Yet my indoctrination into this high-control religion had already begun, and I knew that compliance, even if the situation were scary and unpleasant, would ensure its ending would come sooner.

And it did. After a few sentences about my being mature now, I was told that I needed to accept Jesus Christ as my Lord and Savior to be guaranteed salvation. All I needed to do was say that I was willing to be baptized.

By the time the *z* in *baptized* left his lips, I was saying yes. I needed this experience to be over. A quick prayer with my mother after calling her back into the room, and they were out the door.

It turned out the two strangers were right. They didn't need to remove their overcoats and hats.

The baptism was scheduled for a Sunday immediately following worship service. It was as dry and meaningless as their visit. I had dreaded it up until the moment I went under the water and was more relieved it was all over than at peace that my soul was no longer in peril.

This story is not just a breadcrumb—it's an entire loaf of bread.

Throughout the years, people have shared with me their stories of deconstructing. Most of them sound like mine with experiences throughout our journeys that may have tripped us up for a moment, but we remained loyal to our religious heritage—that is, until one day when we became painfully aware that something was off with our spirituality. Memories from those breadcrumb moments come flooding back, beckoning us to not ignore what was stirring deep inside us for quite some time.

When those breadcrumbs of memories rise, we typically stop denying there is a problem. We then accept the invitation to navigate the spiritual wilderness to seek our spiritual truth. What that spiritual wilderness path looks like will be as vastly different as everyone's spirituality is.

Henry VIII Contributed to My Deconstructing—Seriously

You'll look for the source of your problem anywhere except at the actual place that is the source of your problem.

That thought came to me when I was in seminary. I was doing a journal practice, and the next question was, "What event or events led you to your path of authenticity?" The question was a common one. My seminary class was filled with people deconstructing from evangelical Christianity, and we all shared our stories throughout the two years we were together. I would often share my experiences of being gaslit by church leaders, of feeling empty and disconnected from my religious heritage, of being frustrated by the hypocrisy I witnessed inside the church.

But this day, as I sat alone and felt safe exploring these questions on a deep level, another answer arrived that I had never considered.

King Henry VIII.

Wait. What?

I had never considered how my season of obsession with everything British monarchy had impacted my deconstructing journey, yet here it was arriving in the form of an answer to a seemingly innocuous journaling question. I laughed out loud albeit a little uncomfortably as I thought of how intense my obsession had been.

I mean—intense. Like spending hours at the library intense. Charting British monarchy ancestral diagrams on my basement wall intense. Sitting in on visiting lectures at the university intense.

And as abruptly as it had started, one day the obsession . . . just . . . died. Half-read books sat on my nightstand were unfinished. Diagrams and drawings on my basement wall were abandoned. Reservations to listen to British historian experts were canceled.

As I sat there, amused that Henry VIII was invading this sacred space, I was forced to acknowledge that my intense obsession for and abrupt abandonment of all things royal was a bit strange.

You think?

And just like that, I became aware that I was being invited into another level of untangling from my indoctrination. Did I really want to do this? No, I didn't. My tea was cold, and I was anxious to start my day. But I also knew better. I had been on this deconstructing journey long enough to know that spiritual healing isn't like a shooting star streaking across the sky.

Miss it, and its wisdom may evade me.

Spiritual healing doesn't work that way, though. It arrives when we're ready, inviting us to discover its wisdom. The decision to accept the invitation, however, lies with us. We can receive its wisdom and unlock new understandings about our lived experiences that open pathways to new levels of awareness and healing. We also have the option to turn away from it, refusing to enter the portal, ensuring it'll arrive another day and time as we continue to circle the mountain, insisting that our ways will eventually get us over it.

Except it doesn't, and we are locked into a perpetual pattern of rinse and repeat as we come face-to-face with our shadows and turn away from the healing and wisdom they offer.

I knew this pattern well because I had turned away from these healing portals many times only to find myself exhausted and frustrated as I trudged along in life, carrying the same baggage and tending to the same wounds I had been for a lifetime.

No. This time would be different. I was ready to accept the invitation to discover what an arrogant, egotistical, selfish, entitled man from the sixteenth century had to teach me about my own journey. Warming my tea and resettling into my space, I began to journal about my season obsessing over the British monarchy.

I truly did not see this one coming. Prior to my fascination with the British monarchy, the only things that came close to obsessions for me were rescuing dogs, crocheting, and of course the overcommitment to my church that had me physically at church several times throughout the week, mentally and emotionally connected to the people and the life of the church, and spiritually bound in an unhealthy way.

This was a time in my life when I was in the beginning phases of the spiritual wilderness and found myself still active and present in church.

I may have been physically present in church, but I was faking it in the pews. I was playing a role, a shell of my former passionate self who at one time was so immersed in the life of the church that I didn't know where it ended and my true authentic self began.

I began this phase by reading, learning as much as I could about other Christian denominations' beliefs about Jesus, God, and the Holy Spirit. I dove deeply into mysticism and was so rattled to learn that Christianity had a rich history of it. I still believed that my religious heritage held the answers to my growing sense of spiritual unrest, so much of what I read was Christian-centric. I devoured books by authors such as Rick Warren, Joyce Meyer, and Charles Stanley. I was the proud owner of the entire *Left Behind* series by Tim LaHaye and Jerry Jenkins. Even as a staunch evangelical, I could only make it through the first eight of the sixteen-book series. The storyline became ridiculous, and it wasn't as if I didn't know how it was going to end.

It was during this phase that I sat down one evening to watch *Elizabeth*, starring Cate Blanchett. Cate is one of my favorite actors, and I needed some entertainment after a few intense days. Prior to seeing this movie, I had little desire to dive into the history of the royals. Like most Americans, Diana's tragic story captivated me, especially because she and I are the same age. That captivation never turned into an obsession until I watched Cate bring Queen Elizabeth's story to life.

No doubt timing is everything. Given this was the season of my deconstruction that I was questioning my faith and covertly seeking to find those answers outside the framework of my religious heritage, I could see how the timing of my royals obsession was perfect.

The movie tells the story of Elizabeth Tudor, who becomes queen after her half sister, Queen Mary, dies. Elizabeth, a staunch Protestant, faced dangerous opposition to her reign from adversaries of

the Catholic faith who did not want to lose their power and influence that had been made even more powerful by the reign of
Queen Mary, herself a Catholic. The movie prioritizes the overin-
dulgence of those living within proximity of the queen to increase
its entertainment value. I, however, was transfixed by the storyline
of two queens and two facets of Christianity that would cheat,
deceive, torture, and murder to remain in power.

All in the name of Jesus.

And an obsession was born.

What I remember most profoundly about this season of studying and charting everything about the British monarchy is my family indulging me in this obsession. They sent me articles, bought me
books, asked me questions about my diagrams, and seemed genuinely interested in the work I was doing. When I asked my husband
about why he had been so supportive of my fascination with King
Henry VIII, he simply said that he could tell it was important to me.

Important was an understatement, but I appreciated his being
aware that something was shifting inside me, and on the other
side of King Henry VIII's story was my answer.

Without boring you with the intricate layers of espionage, plot-
ted assassinations, poisonings, horrific abuses of power, and the
occasional authentic love story that is all wrapped up in British
monarchical history, my obsession came to a crashing halt when I
discovered that the Church of England was created for one simple
reason.

Lust.

King Henry VIII's desperate need for a male heir to continue
his dynasty led to a monumental shift in England's religious structure. Despite offers to silence Martin Luther,* a vocal critic of the
Catholic Church, to win the favor of the pope, Henry's request
for an annulment was denied. This meant that he was not free
to divorce Queen Catherine and marry Anne Boleyn, whom he
was certain would produce him the male heir he so desperately
desired.

This denial spurred Henry to launch the English Reformation, creating the Church of England with himself at its head, thereby challenging the pope's authority and altering the power dynamics in England.

The significance of this move was not lost on me. Raised within a patriarchal religious system that rarely addressed the British monarchy or the Church of England, I was astounded to learn the extent of Henry's influence. This realization was jarring, reflecting a deliberate omission by church leaders who likely feared that knowledge of Henry's defiance against the established church might inspire similar rebellion among their congregants. The tale of Henry VIII was more than a historical footnote; it was a testament to the enduring nature of patriarchy and its protective instincts, even as it underscored the transformative power of a single ruler's actions against an established religious order.

I then understood why his story was overlooked in the history of the church.

Church is not God-breathed. It is man-made for man's power. God is an afterthought.

Here I was, reading books from some of the Christian giants whose words now felt hollow and superficial as I sought to reconcile what I thought I knew about my religious heritage to the reality of what it really was.

I soon discovered that the teachings of evangelical Christian-centric teachers like Joyce Meyer and Charles Stanley could do little to settle the unrest I was feeling deep within my soul. They were simply parroting the same patriarchal teachings that had been foundational in my religious conditioning.

Given that I had unlocked a huge clue about Christianity by studying on my own, I began to wonder if I had been looking in the wrong place for answers.

I would need to be careful with this line of thinking and where it might take me. I knew I was already on the radar of church leaders and had been labeled as having a spirit of offense for pushing back on decisions by leadership that seemed to favor those most loyal to the church leaders. And apparently, I wasn't doing a very good job hiding the fact that I was gradually checking out spirituality, because several church friends told me that my "falling away" was the topic of conversation at more than one church meeting.

Nevertheless, as they say, I persisted.

The desire to seek answers to this spiritual unrest outside of my church experience was growing to the point that the risk of being labeled a spiritual troublemaker was worth the journey to discover what lay ahead for me.

Exit King Henry VIII—Enter C. S. Lewis

As children, we were warned about *The Chronicles of Narnia*. We were told it was pagan, it mocked the teachings of the Bible, and it was a gateway for the "devil to get a foothold." As I matured, I came to understand that the devil-foothold thing was a common response when the adults really didn't have an answer, like "because I said so." I was busy with crafts and farm life, so these admonitions kept me away with little disruption in my life of making mud pies, crocheting, and chasing chickens in the barnyard.

It's funny how those admonitions from our childhood stick with us, however, because I remember plainly the feelings that rose within when I came across C. S. Lewis's books in the Christianity section of the library. I felt a sense of defiance as I picked up *The Lion, the Witch and the Wardrobe* and thumbed through it. Immediately, I was taken back to my childhood when I believed there was a devil, and he most likely lived under my bed because I heard things at night.

Fear-based theology really does trip up children, and unless its influence is deconstructed, it lasts into adulthood.

I slowly walked past all of Lewis's books, reading each title and touching each spine gently in almost an act of reverence that would be viewed as heretical by one of my fellow church members had they seen me. By the time I reached the final book on the shelf, I knew one was coming home with me. I just wasn't sure which one. I had steered clear from his writings in my adulthood. It wasn't a cognizant avoidance but most likely residual influence left over from the devil-foothold theology from my childhood hiding just beneath the surface of my spirituality.

Mere Christianity. The book's title intrigued me. How could Christianity ever be considered *mere*? The title felt blasphemous, and that alone was enough for me to grab it, head to the checkout, quickly deposit it into my backpack, and leave before anyone saw me with this book.

I knew that no bona fide, card-carrying evangelical would be caught with one of his books in their homes. Because of that, it was also the first book that I had intentionally kept hidden just in case one of my church members saw it.

From the first page, I was hooked. I loved Lewis's writing style, and every word of the book felt like a homecoming. Lewis gave me permission to view the Bible without the literal lens of my religious heritage. Each chapter beckoned me deeper into the spiritual wilderness, and now I was willingly accepting its call. I finished *Mere Christianity* within days of checking it out and quickly moved to *The Great Divorce* and *The Screwtape Letters.* With each book, I felt a little untangling occurring deep inside me, the loosening of knots to a theology that had held me hostage for most of my life.

Looking back to that season of deconstructing and recalling how defiant I felt toward my religious upbringing seems almost silly. C. S. Lewis is often described as one of the most influential Christian apologists* of the twentieth century. Other apologists have for years used his writings and lectures to defend and articulate the Christian faith. One of Lewis's contemporaries and best friends was J. R. R. Tolkien, a devout Roman Catholic whose faith influenced his worldviews and his world-renowned fantasy novels *The Hobbit* and *The Lord of the Rings.* These were men steeped deeply into organized religion, who defended their faith with a passion unmatched that still reaches up through time to influence us today.

C. S. Lewis is only radical because my religious heritage said he was. In a highly patriarchal system that relies on an unquestioning faith and views church leadership as Divinely appointed, any teacher that encourages individualism* (not to be confused with the ideology of individualism, which I explain in chapter 9) and to seek answers outside of this religious patriarchal structure is seen as a threat and thus labeled heretical. Evangelical leaders equated scholars like Lewis as the boogeyman calling you from inside your home—the danger was lurking from within.

Although C. S. Lewis is clearly not the disruptor that evangelical Christianity made him out to be, reading his books opened the portal into spiritual discovery. Before then, I relied almost exclusively on church leadership for my spiritual direction and guidance. That was, of course, part of the indoctrination of my religious heritage. "Seek pastoral advice" on everything from spirituality to marriage challenges. These religious patriarchal systems demand its congregants' accountability to male church leaders who may or may not have gone to seminary, may or may not have gone to Bible college, and most likely have no training or credentials in counseling.

I mean—what could possibly go wrong?

Still, I was loyal to a fault, seeking advice from my pastors on everything from familial problems to any crisis of faith. Even after some very painful encounters with my pastors and church leaders, where I had been told that I carried a spirit of offense and I needed to search my heart to understand why I was having trouble coming under the authority of the pastors, I continued in this pattern of seeking their advice.

When I was feeling the call to explore formal ministry training, I sought out my pastors for their advice. By this time, C. S. Lewis was on my nightstand, and I was beginning my journey into individualistic spirituality. Yet old habits die hard, and I needed to hear from them on what my next steps should be.

My pastor discouraged me from any training outside of their in-house ministry program. His exact words were, "You don't need seminary. You just need our pastor-in-training program." For the first time in my life, those words filtered through a new reality for me. In other words, they just hit differently, and I could see that the advice I was receiving was what was best for the perpetuity of the church and not necessarily for me.

But my spiritual road map wasn't complete yet, the one that would eventually help me see that the only way to silence the inner voice asking me to dive without reservations into the spiritual wilderness was to leave the church. Without that road map, I still was holding on to some elements of doubt that I was wrong, and my disobedience and questioning of my faith would be punished by God.

My inner child's desire to be seen as the good Christian prevailed. The next week, I enrolled in my church's pastor-in-training program.

My season of faking it in the church pews would continue for several more months. I was living two parallel lives. The good-Christian one found me exhausting myself, overcommitting to committees, event organizing, Bible studies, and church attendance. I had always been a passionate volunteer, but now it took on a whole new level of desperation. I was so desperate to hold on to some element of my religious heritage that I convinced myself that if I just worked harder, my crumbling faith could be revived, and I wouldn't be forced into a decision that I could see coming. My own version of a great divorce from church was off in the distance, and I was terrified that I was spiraling toward it.

With the added work of the pastor-in-training program, it was not uncommon for me to be at church seven days a week.

You read that correctly.

I couldn't imagine my life without my spiritual community, my religious identity, and my religious heritage. I *needed* it as much as it needed me, albeit for entirely different reasons. I believed with every fiber of my being that my spirituality and my salvation were contingent upon my proximity to my keeping the good-Christian label. It's all I had ever known.

The church needed me blindly obedient to the religious patriarchal system to convert more followers to this system to ensure its perpetuity through the financial support that is generated through the tithing system. But this too was all I had ever known. My indoctrination into this system taught me that I had a moral and spiritual obligation to "bring in the sheaves"—more prospects for church membership.

This indoctrination also taught me that the blessings in this life, as well as my spiritual well-being, were directly related to my tithes. Each week, we heard a sermon about how blessings would overflow if we overflowed the offering plate. This is known as *prosperity gospel* or *prosperity theology*, a Christian belief—primarily from the evangelical, apostolic denominations—that donations to one's church will increase one's material wealth and well-being. To say that both aspects of this indoctrination have been a source of spiritual trauma for many people is putting it mildly. Plainly put, the pressure to grow the church falls squarely on church members. If that isn't enough pressure, the sermons on sacrificial giving are a constant drumbeat in the hearts and minds of the faithful.

I've witnessed people not paying their light bill to tithe because they're "believing God for a miracle." Those people are then placed on a pedestal as a living testimony of a faith-filled life.

I'll scream this every chance I get, so here's my moment in this book—prosperity gospel is one of the most toxic tenets of high-control religion.

Untangling from these beliefs is some of the hardest work I've ever done, and at this moment in my deconstruction, I wasn't ready to accept that answering the spiritual wilderness meant that I would be leaving this behind.

That concept seemed not only unfathomable, it also bordered the outrageous.

Seven days a week, Sunday through Saturday, sometimes twice a day, I was at church.

I had my own key to the church so I could come and go as needed. I was trusted, which added to the torment brewing inside me. People relied on me. I was one of just a handful of church leaders on a committee to advise the head pastors. I took my responsibility extremely seriously.

Get it? I *was* the good Christian. Except on the inside, I was anything *but* the good Christian.

I was suffocating, and with each book I read outside of my religious heritage, I was beginning to understand that peace would not be found from within.

My faith was dying, and I had nowhere to go.

C. S. Lewis soothed my soul. He invited me into an intellectual exploration of my faith. His writings transcended Christian authoritarianism.* He taught me that humans have an innate sense of right and wrong that points to a Divine Creator that is nothing like the vengeful, angry God of my religious indoctrination who created me flawed and full of sin. His mastery of allegory* in his fictional writings took the heavy subjects of faith and salvation and offered them in a creative and imaginative way, giving me permission to be curious and not fear my questions that were increasing with each day.

I devoured his writings with an urgency that matched the angst raging just below the surface of my reality. I would play the role of the good Christian at church, only to return home to read the authors my church considered heretical until the wee hours of the morning.

Soon, however, change would once again be on the horizon. There came a familiar desire rising that beckoned me to look beyond what C. S. Lewis had offered. This was the beginning of a familiar pattern that would continue up to my ordination as an interfaith/interspiritual minister in 2017.

The gentle untangling that began with C. S. Lewis would soon become a fierce unraveling that would guide my deconstructing journey for years. That fierce unraveling began when I found the writings of John Shelby Spong.

John Shelby Spong

I don't recall how I discovered him, but to say that his teachings changed my life is an understatement. As I said in chapter 1, I didn't leave his books out on the coffee table for others to see. Besides my husband and my stepdaughter, who was also deconstructing from her faith, I told no one that he was quickly becoming one of my favorite wisdom keepers.

The title of one of his books, *Why Christianity Must Change or Die*, rattled me. Although I was struggling with my faith and desperate to find the answers to my questions and doubts, I simply couldn't imagine a world where Christianity didn't exist.

My relationship with Bishop Spong's books and ideas was a complicated one. *Why Christianity Must Change or Die* stayed tucked inside my desk drawer for months before I finally pulled it out to begin reading. Intuitively, I knew that inside its pages were nuggets of wisdom that I would not be able to unsee or unknow. Like the proverbial apple being eaten by Eve, I recognized that if I read that book, my life would forever be changed.

And I was right.

With every chapter, Bishop Spong gently walked me into a new understanding about my religious heritage. Within that book, he challenged literal interpretations and traditional Christian beliefs that many denominations, mine included, said believing in them was a requirement in order to be a good Christian. He gave compelling arguments on why Christianity must evolve and gave me permission to reexamine a relationship with Jesus that wasn't contingent upon Him[1] dying for my sins.

I was terrified by what I was learning. What if Spong was wrong, and now I was a willing participant in ensuring my spending eternity in hell? What if Jesus was watching over my shoulder and weeping in heaven for my rejecting my religious heritage that said He was everything evangelical Christians said He was? What if my reading these books, which would surely be labeled heretical by my pastors, was the equivalent of denying Christ, the unforgivable sin?

What if I was now the bad Christian, and there was no redemption?

These questions played over and over like a broken record in my mind. As loud as that voice was reminding me that God was watching me and was disappointed in me, there was a louder voice inviting me to trust what was happening and to stay still.

And listen.

And read.

And journal.

And spend time in introspection processing what I was reading.

And then repeating it repeatedly.

Until one day, the regret that I opened the Pandora's box with C. S. Lewis began to be replaced with curiosity as I opened myself up to teachers like Bishop Spong. The fear that I was a bad Christian began to be replaced with inquisitiveness. The anxiety that I was experiencing for considering that my religious heritage was flawed was replaced with . . .

What?

Peace? No. I couldn't call it peace because I was beginning to understand that nothing about my life was ever going to be the same.

Comfort? No. I couldn't call it comfort because the proverbial rug was being jerked out from under me as I began to question everything I had ever been taught in my faith tradition.

Assurance? No. I couldn't call it assurance because I wasn't sure where I was going next or who I would be as I continued to untangle from this toxic theology.*

Betrayal.

Deception.

Disappointment.

Confusion.

Fear.

There it was. That's what I was feeling.

You know the one. The one where you've been living a lie. The one where you thought your life was this one way, but it wasn't even close. Those of us who have experienced a profound sense of betrayal understand this.

I pray that isn't you and that it is only through these words that you are understanding what this betrayal is like.

There would be no turning back now.

There would be no unseeing.

This would never be unknown.

This was who I was now.

A deconstructing evangelical Christian who didn't know where to turn or whom to trust.

Unchurched with No Spiritual Road Map

Eventually, the trust I once had for my church leaders shifted to those I was discovering in the books I read and the videos I watched. Many of those authors and teachers were themselves former evangelical Christians who had deconstructed some aspect of their religious heritage. Some remained in the church, like Bishop Spong, Rachel Held Evans, author of *A Year of Biblical Womanhood*, and Barbara Brown Taylor, author of *Leaving Church*. Some deconstructed to agnosticism* or atheism,* like Bart Ehrman, author of *How Jesus Became God*. Still, some converted to other religions, like Reza Aslan, author of *Zealot: The Life and Times of Jesus of Nazareth*.

And me?

Deconstructing spiraled me completely out of organized Christianity to become an unchurched, nonconforming Christian who is an ordained interfaith/interspiritual minister. It doesn't fit nicely on a business card, but it serves my purpose of identifying who I am.

Although I am unchurched and my faith looks nothing like the beliefs I was taught from my religious heritage, I hold on to my Christian identity for a number of reasons, primarily because I did the work to become a Christian.

I've been baptized twice. I tithed almost my entire life until I deconstructed. I volunteered countless hours of unpaid labor at any church I attended. I served in leadership and was responsible for launching creative initiatives for youth, young adults, and even adult Bible studies.

More importantly, I embodied my faith with passion and action. I rarely missed Sunday school, and I always had my study Bible, my prayer journal, and my latest church project covering my kitchen table.

I walked, talked, and lived my faith.

Then I had a huge realization: no one has the authority to toss me out of the Christian club. I used to believe that church leaders held that power. Yes, a church member can be excommunicated and your church membership can be revoked, but the identity of Christians expands far beyond the reach of church leaders who act as if they alone hold the keys to Christendom.

But let us ask ourselves who sits in a position of authority for *all* of Christianity to label me unworthy? Who gets to tell me that I am not a Christian? Who is the gatekeeper of the entirety of Christianity to pronounce me a heretic?

Who?

There are over thirty-five thousand Christian denominations, and the last time I checked, not one denomination or leader has authority over all these denominations (although some like to pretend they do!). It's also important to note that the reason all these denominations exist . . . is because they could not agree on scriptural interpretation, leadership, or biblical authority.

Well, this just got awkward, didn't it?

Let's all thank Martin Luther for that. Without the courage to resist the authority of the Catholic Church in the sixteenth century, we'd all be observing Mass and baptizing our babies. Not that there is anything wrong with that if those beliefs enrich your spiritual journey.

You know what I mean.

Church leaders' responses to those of us deconstructing range from those who are accusing the deconstructing Christian of being a heretic, to church leaders who support those of us deconstructing, welcome our questions and doubts, and even encourage our leaving organized religion if it serves us on our spiritual journeys.

Our deconstructing journeys do not need validation by church leaders to be authentic, but they also don't deserve to be criticized by them.

We need the space to explore our spiritual journeys.

Our courage to do so should be respected.

The Scary Side of Deconstructing

It isn't uncommon, however, for those deconstructing to find themselves in a season of desperation and panic. I struggled with feelings of guilt for what I viewed as my abandoning the religion of my heritage and mounting fear that I had somehow jeopardized my salvation. Outside of my husband, who had supported my decision and left the church at the same time I did, there was no one I could share my feelings of guilt and fear. Two of our children remained at the church, and it was important to us that our decision to leave did not sway them from their spiritual journeys.

I'm grateful that I trusted this deconstructing journey enough to work through those feelings of spiritual wobbliness and dive into the work of deconstructing.

Believing in this process is what brought me to where I am today. I still call myself an unchurched, nonconforming Christian, but I now add "who walks the spiritual but not religious path." That is the best way to describe my spiritual authenticity after deconstructing my faith. But that is my journey through deconstructing my faith. Yours may be entirely different. In fact, *expect* it to be entirely different. Just like any other healing process, if you hold as your intention "the highest good for all involved" instead of focusing on what you think the outcome will be, you will be amazed at what arrives for the next phase of your spiritual journey.

Factors That May Impact Deconstructing Your Faith

Deconstructing your faith is about a willingness to come face-to-face with your religious indoctrination, most likely the only funnel through which you have sought an understanding of spirituality. An important first step in deconstructing is to explore how your life's journey has played a role in shaping not only your values and beliefs but also your biases and prejudices. You may be unaware at this time what some of those factors are. Don't worry—if you are committed to fully examining all the ways that your environment helped shape your beliefs and values, you will discover the ones that may be hidden from you at this moment.

That is the sacred and healing wisdom found in diving fully into the work of deconstruction. Earlier in this chapter I mentioned a few factors that may play a role in shaping your beliefs and values:

→ Religious heritage
→ Cultural and family values
→ Life experiences
→ Demographic characteristics

A good first step is to begin a deconstructing-your-faith journal and write who in each of the above categories had great influence over you. For instance, for religious heritage, my grandmother played a huge role in indoctrinating me into Southern Baptist theology. However, she also holds the space in my family values for instilling in me a desire to be curious, to be unafraid to ask questions, and to believe in myself when others do not. Another example would be my geographic location because growing up in small midwestern towns played a huge role in my limited understanding of the world.

This simple journaling exercise can be helpful as you begin this journey. It can hold clues for the beginning line of deconstruction. For now, let's visit each factor and consider other ways that they may have impacted your life.

Religious Heritage

Many of my followers on social media share a similar religious heritage as mine and are deconstructing what is often described as mainstream, or "modern," evangelical Christianity. The word *modern* is in quotes because to label evangelical Christianity as modern is an oxymoron. *Modern* simply refers to the rebranding of worship style and marketing tactics (like pastors in jeans) to infer a liberated theology, when nothing is further from the truth. Fear-based theology is foundational to many evangelical churches, regardless of how they market themselves. Fear-based theology invokes the fear of hell or being left behind when the rapture occurs to demand obedience to that church's interpretation of scripture. Deconstructing from fear-based theology can be extremely challenging, especially when your experience included weaponizing not only fear but guilt and shame.

Challenging but not impossible. Even after ten years of actively deconstructing my own religious heritage, a slight pang of guilt may arise on a Sunday morning as I recall my life before deconstruction. The important thing to remember is that the work of deconstructing your religious heritage starts with a commitment to peel back all the many layers that comprise your indoctrination from that religious experience.

While many of us are deconstructing from evangelical Christianity, there are others who are deconstructing from other Christian denominations, including Catholicism, as well as non-Christian religions. This falling away from religion will be covered in more depth in chapter 5. For now, it's important to recognize your religious heritage as the starting point for your deconstruction.

This is why I recommend journaling as part of your deconstruction journey. Unpacking what your religious indoctrination taught you to believe allows you to reflect on those beliefs and how they have impacted your life. We are often the keepers of wisdom that will help guide us on our healing journeys.

The important thing to remember is that your indoctrinated beliefs from your religious heritage—regardless of your denominational experience—can significantly impact you. Be open to examining them so that your life is free from indoctrinated biases and prejudices as well as beliefs that do not serve your highest good.

Culture and Family Values

While religion can be the teacher of some of your prejudices and biases of other humans, your cultural and family values can also impact how you deconstruct from your religious heritage. By being open to exploring what you were taught in your homelife about the value of humans that do not look like, love like, believe like, or vote like you do, you have a greater chance of discovering how your religious indoctrination either complicated or collided with your familial values.

Oftentimes these beliefs and values are one and the same—what you heard in church was what you heard in your home. Sometimes, however, there may be a more radical view of the world that greatly impacts how you view others who are different from you. These views can also influence your political affiliations as well as your work in social justice and activism.

Another important reason for examining your family beliefs and values as part of your deconstruction journey is because the chances of your relationship with loved ones being impacted by your deconstruction are very good. Many of us who have deconstructed our religious heritage discovered that some of our relationships with loved ones and friends improved as we became more aligned politically and spiritually. Conversely, there were some that have become strained and, sadly, even nonexistent.

This brutal truth—that your relationships may change, and some may fall away—can be frightening, especially as you consider the number of ways that deconstruction is impacting you spiritually, mentally, and emotionally. This is why deconstruction should be given the time and commitment it needs to be done with sacred intention and purpose. I'm not at all suggesting that the objective is to change your relationships, but this is the time to examine them and see how the ones that are meaningful may—or perhaps should—change.

All too often we stay silent in the presence of forced ideologies within our inner circles, which should be where the most sacred and meaningful relationships live. Instead, we've allowed a person or group of people to dominate our narrative while we stay silent and suffer under their beliefs about how our lives should look.

Shouldn't deconstruction from our faith include an element of deconstructing from anything that no longer serves our highest good? By doing the practice of simply examining how cultural or family values and beliefs have impacted you, you are not making any decisions about those relationships. It just helps you define how you came to be where and who you are today.

Life Experiences

I've been posting on social media for many years. Although I considered myself experienced in the social media game, nothing prepared me for going viral on TikTok. Even though the platform appeals to a younger audience, I just surpassed 670,000 followers across several social medial platforms at the time of this writing, and the follower count is still growing. Engagement with my followers is what makes the time commitment worth it. Even the negative comments provide an opportunity for dialogue that teaches and empowers our followers.

One of the first videos that went viral on TikTok was about affirming the LGBTQIA+ community to live authentically without the fear of sin or eternal damnation. Almost immediately after posting it, someone responded, "Although I'm an atheist, I grew up reading the Bible, and being gay is a sin. Stop lying to people."

While it isn't uncommon to receive comments saying that the Bible says being gay is a sin (for the record, it isn't), I found it interesting that someone who identified as an atheist felt the need to state his nonbelief while defending this homophobic interpretation of scripture.

That is basically what I said to this person, and his response back was even more perplexing. He became very defensive and insulting, insisting that he couldn't care less about the harm it does the LGBTQIA+ community. He reiterated that if they're gay, they're going to hell because being gay is a sin. He ended one comment with, "The truth is the truth."

Each time he commented, I returned to my original question of why he, a self-proclaimed atheist, felt the need to comment on a video that was about helping the LGBTQIA+ community heal from religious trauma. He refused to explain and apparently became frustrated with my asking him to elaborate because he deleted his comments and blocked me.

Demographic Characteristics

Since that experience, I've encountered similar situations with people who have left church but doubled down on their interpretation of scripture and how it applies to our lives today. When these commenters are open to answering my questions, I find that all of them have had bad experiences inside Christianity that led to their exodus from the church.

While many of them have said they "deconstructed" from religion, which led to their now identifying as spiritual but not religious, agnostic, or atheist, most of them could not quantify their deconstruction process beyond "leaving church." These conversations with followers are but a small sampling of those who are deconstructing, yet they reveal how indoctrinated religious beliefs may still impact their lives outside of Christianity.

I am typing this as I'm actively monitoring comments on a video I recently posted. Someone said she was glad she deconstructed from religion because she feels freer than ever before. However, she is sad that she will not see her family in heaven and has accepted that she's going to hell.

I know all too well that fear of hell and eternal damnation. It kept me bound to a fear-based theology as I repeatedly tried to find my way inside a religion that was beginning to feel too small and restrictive for who I was becoming. That fear of hell wasn't enough to keep me from leaving, but I remember having waves of fear that I had just sealed my fate of burning forever in a lake of fire when I died.

When I began my deconstruction journey, I knew I no longer wanted to be bound to this theology and entrenched in fear, and I wanted to untangle who I was becoming from the beliefs that held me captive. For me, that meant becoming a voracious reader of scholars and sages to understand the Bible outside the construct of my religious heritage. As I read and studied the historical context surrounding ancient scripture and learned about alternative Christian theologies, my layers of indoctrinated beliefs began to peel away. That included my fear of eternal damnation.

Let me be clear about what I'm saying. Your beliefs are your beliefs. Deconstructing can take many different forms, and the result can be different for each person. It doesn't mean that you *must* reject all your beliefs—it simply means that you are open to examining them and their power over you. While there are no hard-and-fast rules about what it will look like or how long it will take, deconstructing should include a peeling back of indoctrinated beliefs to see them outside the construct of your religious heritage.

Without this work of deconstructing, there is a risk of holding on to biases and prejudices that will continue to impact how you are showing up in the world. And how we show up in the world is what I believe is one of the most critical elements of spirituality.

I think of the people I've encountered on social media who now live outside of church yet continue to condemn others to a hell that they supposedly don't believe in. I think of the vitriol they hurl at me as I offer a mirror into their hypocrisy. They simply refuse to open their eyes and see how their own religious indoctrination has manifested as anger and judgment.

I think of my own deconstruction journey that found me on the floor and crying many times as I grieved the loss of my religious heritage. I'm grateful to my mentors who lovingly guided me through spiritual care and a shedding of those beliefs that had me convinced that as a Christian I was superior, and outside of Christianity were those doomed to a fiery hell.

I think of the thousands of people who are actively doing the work of deconstructing. The ones asking incredible, life-changing questions, engaging with and supporting one another throughout their own journeys. Every day, I receive messages from people sharing their gratitude for helping them on their deconstructing journeys for giving them hope that peace and happiness can happen after leaving their religious heritage.

Arguing with people who cannot see that rejecting their religious heritage is not the same as deconstructing it has proven to be a fruitless effort. It's also left me exposed to people who resort to attacking me instead of considering that their views are still deeply entrenched in toxic theology.

I no longer waste my time engaging with people who have rejected Christianity but have not deconstructed it. It isn't because I don't care—I do. The reality is that there is only so much time in a day filled with helping people who truly desire it and are committed to doing the hard work.

This chapter is an invitation to consider what beliefs are hiding in the deep recesses of your past or even perhaps your wounds from Christianity. Declining this invitation may be pointing you to your own blind spots of biases and prejudices you are protecting. Rejecting without reflecting on how religion has impacted and continues to impact your views and perceptions may be inhibiting your healing.

A final word of encouragement: as challenging as this may sound, do not worry about what you are deconstructing *toward*, who you will become, or what you will believe. Some people cannot imagine that deconstructing leads them to atheism. Even deconstructing out of the church is unimaginable for some. But if I could encourage you with one thing, it is this: I've never met anyone who regretted deconstructing.

Ever.

Some of us are carrying so many layers of limited beliefs due to our indoctrinations from religious, familial, and societal patriarchy that we have no idea about who we are when we are free from them. Deconstructing invites your authentic self to the table, to dance, and to live free without the suffocating constraints of forced narratives about what others think you *should* be.

I never imagined I'd be unchurched.

The journey that brought me to this place taught me who I am. It also brought me some of my life's greatest mentors and teachers. For all of them, I remain forever grateful.

Deconstructing from Christianity is hard soul work.

That work can begin with your answering one question: "What inside me needs to be healed so I can show up in my life as a better version of myself?"

Then do that work. In the end, it's worth it.

Beloved,

Demolish. Repair. Restore.
  Think about a time in your life when you knew something was fundamentally wrong, yet you chose to ignore it.
  Hoping it would get better by some miracle.

Crossing your fingers that the noise coming from the engine didn't signal anything too expensive.

Praying that the leak in the roof didn't get any bigger and cause a deluge in your living space.

And how often did we know that hoping, crossing our fingers, and praying didn't work for us?

This is the lesson in this chapter. This is a message of affirmation—your doubts, your questions, your being curious about exploring other aspects of faith were not delusions. They were real and were pointing you to your spiritual truth.

Perhaps you were like I was—praying that my faith would be enough, and I wouldn't have to deconstruct from my religious heritage to find who I really was.

Those prayers invited me to look critically at my journey to show me that who I was becoming was who I was always intended to be.

It isn't uncommon to fear that we are making a mistake when we begin to deconstruct. But let me assure you that demolishing that which is binding you to a theology that no longer serves your highest good will allow you to find freedom in ways that were not available inside your religious heritage. Use the following journaling prompts in a way that serves your healing journey.

REFLECTIVE QUESTIONS AND JOURNALING PROMPTS

→ *When looking back at your life, can you identify moments when your actions or beliefs diverged from the religious teachings you received? How did those moments make you feel about your faith?*

→ *Reflect on the story of King Henry VIII's break from the Catholic Church. How does his bold move challenge or reinforce your understanding of spiritual authority and the right to question religious structures?*

➜ *How have the writings of thinkers like C. S. Lewis or John Shelby Spong resonated with or challenged your personal beliefs? What specific ideas or passages have stuck with you, and why?*

TIMELINE EXERCISE

➜ *Add to your timeline where you can recall any memory where you learned something that shook your reality or a foundational truth. Don't overthink this. This may be something that challenged your faith but also changed your perception about your world and how you fit into it. Oftentimes, those experiences when put together reveal a path that has brought you to a place where you are ready to revisit indoctrinated beliefs.*

This is why you are reading this book.

3

Patriarchy "Mansplained"

Being Set Free from Internalized Patriarchy
in the Church and in Our Family

A gentle warning—this chapter discusses anorexia.

I love sitting outdoors to write.

One day while sitting at a coffee shop writing, I noticed a man out of the corner of my eye standing and staring at me. It was an odd sensation because he was close enough—five or so feet—to make his presence known by shifting his weight and folding his arms in front of his chest.

My first thought was, *This man is annoyed with me.* Even in those few seconds before raising my eyes to meet his, my brain was cycling through what I could have done in the hour I had been sitting there.

Was I sitting at his favorite table?

Did I cut him off in line?

When my eyes met his, my suspicions were correct. He was annoyed, and I sat waiting for him to explain what harm I had done to create such a response from him.

He put his hands on his hips and simply said . . .

"Smile."

My response?

Without hesitation. Without thinking. Without checking in

with the parts of me that were screaming that this whole experience was highly problematic and offensive . . .

I smiled.

And with a little nod of satisfaction as if to say, "Good girl," he
turned and began to walk away.

I watched him leave the patio, get in his car, and drive away.
He never even looked in my direction again.

Just like that, he was gone.

What the hell had just happened?

But I was so shaken and so—what? Violated? Was that the
right word? No, that couldn't be. Could it? Why not?

I felt so humiliated and emotional that it was all I could do to
pack up my computer and grab my latte without dropping one or
both while walking to the car.

I replayed the entire experience in my head. I vacillated between
anger toward myself for having been so gullible to blind rage toward this man who felt entitled enough to interrupt a woman sitting quietly, obviously engrossed in her work.

Why was I having such a raw and emotional reaction to this?

With time, that experience has become less raw, but its lesson
about the callousness of some men and the indoctrinations that
teach women to submit to male authority has stayed with me.

And the name of this kind of indoctrination?

Patriarchy.

Think You're Not Impacted by Patriarchy? Think Again.

One thing I didn't share about this experience is my age when it
occurred. This didn't happen to me in my twenties, thirties, or
even forties.

I was fifty-four. Right smack-dab in the middle of my deconstruction. I had been unchurched for several years prior to this
and was preparing to enter seminary. I was deep into doing the
hard work of deconstructing from toxic theology and patriarchal
indoctrinations.

Looking back, I think that is one of the reasons my response was so emotional. After all the work that I had done, that singular experience with a stranger showed me how deep these indoctrinated beliefs live in us.

Eventually, I would be able to see that day at the coffee shop as a gift. It pointed me to the places where the wounds from patriarchy were still living inside me, and it was time to move into another level of healing.

Whether it's religious, familial, or societal—it's patriarchy.

It's important to define patriarchy to fully understand its impact on our lives.

A simple definition of patriarchy is "a form of social organization in which the father is the supreme authority in the family, clan, or tribe and descent is reckoned in the male line."[1] This definition implies that patriarchy can only be found within the familial framework, but it is prevalent in education and political systems—and of course organized religion.

Patriarchal structures prioritize the importance of male leadership and reinforce gender roles and stereotypes that perpetuate the notion that all others within this structure should be subordinate to the chosen male leadership. Historically, the emphasis has been on the negative impact that patriarchy has had on women. However, anyone who is not at the top of the patriarchal structure, meaning all others who are not cisgender,* will ultimately feel the impacts of this oppressive system.

Men are seen as the ultimate authority or decision-maker, with all others within that familial, religious, or societal structure expected to submit to their rule. This is where the intersection of oppression that leads to sexism, racism, and classism can be seen and experienced by the historically oppressed.

To ensure its perpetuity, reinforcement of the importance of the patriarchal structure is a critical element. These reinforcement tactics lead to highly orchestrated indoctrinations that begin early within that framework.

For example, children in high-control patriarchal familial

structures are instructed to view their father as an authoritarian figure. These children have little to no resources for pushing
back on the father's decisions, where any type of questioning his
authority would be seen as disrespectful and argumentative. In
situations where the father resorts to intimidation, bullying, or,
even worse, abuse, the spouse and other adults in the home will
often make excuses for the father's behavior, further reinforcing
his authority. This behavior by the other adults reflects their own
indoctrination into the patriarchal structure, which we'll expand
on later in this chapter.

While children are often exposed to patriarchal indoctrinations in their home, it isn't uncommon that they encounter these
indoctrinations in their educational experience. For instance, my
education was in the '60s and '70s, and primarily in Kentucky
and Indiana, where evangelical conservative beliefs influenced
the education of children. The curriculum I experienced focused
heavily on a male-centric emphasis that prioritized their stories of
leadership, bravery, and innovation. Gender roles were reinforced
inside this educational structure, where my only option for electives in high school concentrated on trades that were traditionally
held by women. From sewing, cooking, home budgets, and caring
for children, I emerged a well-rounded woman with the excep-
tional skill of matching my plaids on the final sewing project of
my junior year—a plaid skirt. Although I received high marks for
the sewing of this skirt, I ultimately received an F on the project.
Why? Because I refused to wear the skirt to school, which was a
requirement for the project to be graded.

In high school, I was five feet nine inches tall and weighed 105
pounds. If size 0 would have been a thing in the '70s, I would
have worn it. It was a regular occurrence for someone to call me
beanpole or *anorexic*. I looked like the former. It was the latter that
always hurt the worst because it implied that I somehow was contributing to my physique by refusing to eat. I ate ample amounts
of carbs and proteins, but my physique never changed, and I was
mortified by my skinny legs. My knees protruded significantly. The

very short cheerleading skirts didn't help that, but thankfully in the '70s, knee socks with cheer outfits were not only a thing, they were also fashionable. Sadly, I had no boots or socks that matched the plaid skirt. Instead of enduring another round of ridicule for my skinny legs, I opted to receive a failing grade for a near-perfect handmade skirt.

The fact that sewing and home economics were my only options for electives clearly reflects a patriarchal structure that reinforced a girl's value in who she would become as a "helpmate" to her husband someday. It would be easy to miss the patriarchal influence swirling in my experience with being ridiculed for how I looked and how the quality of my work could only be appreciated through my submitting to a ridiculous rule about my needing to wear the skirt. Patriarchy never celebrates individualism and perceives it as a threat. All must comply, lest they suffer the consequences because patriarchy not only selectively chooses your education, it tells you what to wear and to be silent in the face of judgment and mockery.

It never occurred to me until years later that my refusing to wear the skirt was a moment of my resisting this patriarchal indoctrination. I would be much older before becoming aware of this. Still, in later life, I obviously carried deep within me those indoctrinated teachings and without thinking would obey an annoyed man who demanded that I smile at his command to do so.

Patriarchy believes that those in the top tier of this structure mandate the normative standards for everyone. This is how bigoted beliefs and ideologies are born. Because if you do not look like, love like, or believe like, or if you were not born in the same place as the dominant male, then you are undervalued in those societies.

Just like its counterparts of familial and educational patriarchy, religious patriarchy centers the male experience, authorship, and leadership. A church or denomination that does not ordain women as pastors and limits the roles women can play in church leadership is one that is structured under a patriarchal model.

But women in leadership roles inside the church is but one example of how patriarchy might impact the lives of women. Even in churches that ordain women, patriarchy often will be prevalent, demanding a strict structure that is unspoken but most assuredly present. I witnessed this in some of the more progressive-leaning churches. The men in leadership would often resort to mansplaining,* condescension, or even outright intimidation if the decision at hand was not going in the direction they wanted.

Men in leadership resorting to intimidation to influence a decision reflects how severely patriarchy can impact all of us. What this means is that those indoctrinated into some elements of patriarchy must be willing to do the hard work of deconstructing from these indoctrinations to be not only an ally* but a helpful one who contributes positively and amplifies the voices of the historically oppressed.

As disturbing as it was to witness this abuse of power in high-control, evangelical churches, as well as progressive churches, equally disturbing are those of us who were aware of or, even worse, witnessed this abuse of power and chose to remain silent. The choice to not call out these abuses reflects our own indoctrinations from patriarchal influences. Religious patriarchy taught us that church authority was ordained by God, which meant questioning church leaders was akin to disrespecting God. Many of us also witnessed what happened to the poor souls who decided to tempt fate and challenge patriarchal authority, only to witness them being rebuked, stripped of positions of leadership, or even in some cases asked to leave the church entirely. It became the wiser choice to keep our heads down and stay silent for the sake of "keeping the peace" than to challenge it and risk the assault being turned toward us.

Remaining silent often became a choice of survival for many of us, and I'm sure my story resonates with you on some level, especially if you are a baby boomer or Gen Xer.

This is an intentional part of the indoctrination—to convince you that your worth and your identity are only valid based on your connection to and approval of the church. When the entirety of your identity is wrapped up in your church, the thought of losing that identity and community made speaking out against patriarchal abuses too great a risk.

Silence became necessary for survival for many of us—that is, until one day, for me at least, the risk of drowning in the words that I had been swallowing for years became too great . . .

Then I opened my mouth, and the words poured out of me.

I had been a church administrator long enough to see the harmful patterns, and I could no longer stay silent.

I called out favoritism, hypocrisy, toxic theology that was harmful to the LGBTQIA+ community, people who had been put in positions of power because of their loyalty to church leaders regardless of their experience, questionable practices that hid how pastors were ordained within the church, and unethical financial practices that kept confidential the church's finances and staff salaries.

What was the result of all of those words that finally spilled out of me? I was told that I had a spirit of offense, that I needed to submit to church leadership, and that I was in jeopardy of losing my leadership role. Sermons were written targeting me, prompting church members to seek me out after service, concerned about how blatantly I was being called out in those sermons. Interestingly but not surprisingly, those people concerned about me never went to the pastor to complain about his behavior.

Remember—silence becomes necessary for survival, and those who chose to remain silent had just witnessed what happens when one speaks out against patriarchal abuses.

I didn't know it then, but the first stages of my active deconstructing began the minute I found my voice. A few months later, I would be walking out of those church doors for good, leaving church leadership to scramble to get "ahead of the story" by announcing that I was leaving because I was too sympathetic to "homosexuals."

Whatever that means.

The church leaders' spin on my leaving the church was enough to appease most of the people who were firmly indoctrinated into religious patriarchy and would not dare question leadership or rise to defend me, even though many felt that the leadership had caused tremendous harm to me in their attempts to force me to submit to church authority. The desire to speak up may have been there, but weighing it against the cost confirmed the risk was too great.

And the risk? Rejection.

Now, standing on the outside of those church doors, I understood fully what it meant to be rejected. I knew I could never "go home" unless I was willing to acquiesce to a system that I found suffocating and toxic.

For me, the rejection was worth it. But it would take time for me to say that. Time for me to deconstruct and understand how deeply patriarchal indoctrinations had harmed me.

The use of male-gendered language and imagery in the Bible reinforces the idea that men are primarily the chosen gender for leadership. The biblical stories focus on male characters, with women assigned secondary roles or, even in some cases, eliminating the female voices and perspectives altogether.[2]

Each time I share a story about how my voice had been repeatedly silenced by male church leaders, it resonates deeply with my followers. They share similar stories of being chastised, even ridiculed or mocked for believing that they have personal agency over their bodies and their minds. Women will tell how church leaders demanded they submit to church authority and apologize for their "sin" of stepping out of line when they spoke their minds or defied church authority in any way.

Especially prevalent in the conservative, fundamentalist side of Christianity is the notion that it is not scriptural for women to be leaders in the church. These churches also teach that women should be subservient to male leadership in the home as well as in church.

With some regularity, I will have people demand of me to

answer, "Under whose male authority are you preaching?" While there may be an appearance of elements of modernity in conservative churches that ordain women, it's questions like these that reflect the real belief that women's worth as leaders is only validated through the men who put them in that role. This once again is another indoctrinated belief that is rooted in a patriarchal structure. A name for this type of belief system is *complementarian theology** — the belief that men and women are assigned distinct gender roles by God, and men ultimately hold authority over all humans.

When I first began to teach on social media, I often would try to answer the question, "Under whose male authority are you preaching?" I soon learned that outside of my submitting my ministry to an actual man and my teachings being reviewed and approved by him (because this is literally the definition of complementarian theology), I was never going to be labeled anything other than an apostate* by the people who disapproved of my ministry. I have since learned that it is far better to honor my authenticity and be labeled an apostate by those who disapprove of me than to be found acceptable by a theology that I rejected wholeheartedly and with passion.

I am proof that you can heal from religious patriarchy.

Think You Haven't Benefited from Patriarchy? Think Again.

In a *New York Times* article published on March 19, 2019, Maya Salam compared patriarchy to the movie *Terminator 2*—the scenes where the bad Terminator, no matter how many times it was smashed, shot, or run over, just kept coming back as an unstoppable force. Salam said, "That's the patriarchy." It's a somewhat comical comparison but a sad reflection of an archaic, oppressive system that continues to persist no matter how many of us scream about its dangers.

As we have seen, patriarchy is found everywhere—in familial, educational, political, governmental, and religious systems—and it is always about protecting the privilege,* control, and power of the male leadership. It relies on systems of oppression that systemically keep the marginalized undereducated, underresourced, underrepresented, and undervalued.

Patriarchal structures offer those in the higher echelon of a patriarchal system the most power. While the ultimate power is in a man's control—specifically a white, cisgendered, able-bodied, heterosexual, Christian man here in America—anyone in proximity to that power has benefited from that patriarchal structure.

And who are those people within the proximity of that power? You and I.

This may be one of many uncomfortable truths for some of you, but let us not shy away from facing them. Understanding how we benefited from the patriarchal structures within our lives will help us deconstruct not only the harm they caused but also the perceived power we may be holding on to. Each day, I celebrate the former with hundreds of people doing the hard work of deconstruction. Sadly, however, I also cringe as yet another person who "thinks" they're doing the work of deconstruction doubles down as they try desperately to hold on to the belief that they wield some sort of power over others.

Let's dive into this uncomfortable truth and be at once healed and relieved from these toxic beliefs.

When I say that you and I benefit from this patriarchal structure, I'm speaking of those of us whose proximity to power aided us in our lives. Admitting that we had an advantage because of that proximity doesn't minimize the fact that we may have challenges related to real-life issues like housing, employment, or even food security. My mother, who was divorced from my father when I was six years old, often worked two jobs to make ends meet. We never went without food or a roof over our heads, but my brother and I knew we were poor. We rarely ate out, and there were a few times that heat for our home had to wait until the next paycheck.

Hard times were prevalent within our family structure as well as in the communities in which we lived in Kentucky and Indiana.

Most people in our immediate family and in our neighborhoods lived paycheck to paycheck. Layoffs at one job meant someone may be going without supper by the following week.

Times were indeed tough. So you'd be hard-pressed to convince someone who feels like life is constantly kicking them that they have somehow benefited from a patriarchal structure when they are still living in the same trailer that they inherited from their parents. Poverty seems to pass down to the next generation.

But the truth, as it often is, is lying just below the surface if we're willing to look a little deeper into the structure and how we benefited from its existence.

The first uncomfortable truth lies in the actual patriarchal structure itself because it is built upon white supremacy.* A poor white person will still experience preferential treatment in everyday situations, from how they are treated at the grocery store to how schoolteachers speak to them. Black, Indigenous, and People of Color experience acts of racist microaggression* in ways that their poor white counterparts do not.

Historically and sadly still prevalent today, white people are far more likely to be hired for a job compared to a Black applicant with the same qualifications.[3] Racism knows no financial barriers, and Black people still fare far worse than white people on all measurable outcomes, including access to health care, housing, and education.

What this uncomfortable truth means for me is that as hard as my childhood may have been, Black people in this country always had it worse, and in some instances, severely worse.

As a child of the '60s and '70s growing up in southern Indiana, I became aware of what racism was as I matured. I remember a few road signs that "informed" passersby that we were passing through a sundown town—a town or neighborhood that used racist policies and intimidating tactics to exclude and discriminate against nonwhite individuals.[4] I knew how adults felt about the Black people in our community. I heard it every day—in school, at home, and even on the playground. Some of us were told not to play with the Black students. I didn't understand why, but I was deep in my own indoctrination and doing whatever I could be to be seen as the good girl. I had figured out early on that compliance meant approval, and I desperately needed to be validated.

I remained silent, as did my fellow students, neighbors, and family members. We weren't necessarily bad people. We were simply exemplifying what we saw as "just the way it was" in that time in America. No one saw the need to change it, at least not in our neighborhoods. Our proximity to the top of that power structure meant we enjoyed a level of safety and security that didn't motivate us to scoot over and allow others to climb closer to the top. After all, their gain shouldn't be at our expense.

That uncomfortable truth—that we somehow were threatened by another person's advancement—is an integral part of patriarchal indoctrination. This belief ensures that those clamoring for safety and security within that structure view one another as adversaries, not allies. This benefits those in power because no one is talking about the true source of their pain—the patriarchal structure itself.

Once I became aware of how racist and sexist this Americanized version of patriarchal structures is, I carried much guilt with me for my lack of understanding and empathy throughout my childhood. Of course, I could rationalize it that I was indeed a child. How could I possibly have known better when my entire existence was immersed in patriarchal beliefs? And within those beliefs, I never heard from a teacher that we white people needed to change how we treated Black people, Indigenous people, and People of Color. I never heard a sermon about civil rights and the need for social change.

I was never taught within my familial structure that these patriarchal systems benefited those of us at the top because of the color of our skin.

It was when I knew better that I did better. The work that I do to untangle those patriarchal indoctrinations is some of the hardest but most rewarding work on my deconstructing journey.

Becoming aware that the structure exists and that we as white people benefit greatly from that structure is the first step in deconstructing from it.

It's some of the most challenging work that you will do, but it is worth it.

Even after reading this, there will be naysayers who do not believe the data that supports this uncomfortable truth. They will double down on what they perceive as an inherent right to be the keeper of heteronormative standards. They will be the ones captured on video, immortalized for their entitlement as they scream to a Black person, demanding answers to statements like:

"Do you live here? If so, prove it!"

"Hey, you can't park there! Everyone knows that's my spot!"

"What are you doing walking in my neighborhood?"

On and on it goes with an infinite supply of videos capturing those who are desperately trying to hold on to an archaic system that the world is rapidly rejecting. They've come to be known by the name of *Karen*, a slang term that typically refers to a white woman who is displaying entitlement and demanding behavior, which is most oftentimes racist and confrontational.

There is another term for this behavior.

It is also known as *carrying water** for the patriarchy.

Think You're Not Carrying Patriarchy? Think Again.

I sometimes wonder if people grow tired of how often I teach about the impact patriarchy has had on our lives. In this chapter, we have discussed how familial and religious patriarchy indoctrinated us to believe in our moral and spiritual superiority. It also taught us to submit to the white, Christian, cisgender, male authority.

We remained silent even when their actions were hypocritical and harmful.

But why?

Why would we remain silent?

Why wouldn't we use our voices to speak up and push back on toxic indoctrinated beliefs when they hurt so many people?

Our silence can arise from two places.

The first is somewhat complicated, as we discussed above. If our indoctrination is all we know, then we may not even be aware that we are complicit in an oppressive system that harms those low in the patriarchal structure. Even if we are aware of it, so powerful are these indoctrinated beliefs that we may not be able to comprehend life without this structure in place. We also adhere to the limiting beliefs about our humanity that patriarchy teaches. The thought of giving up our identity—even if it is suffocating our ability to reach our full potential—is too scary, and so we stay committed to and a victim of patriarchy.

The more sinister of the two is the second reason some of us do not push back on toxic patriarchal indoctrinations. It is because we enjoy our proximity to power and will actively work to ensure its survival for our own selfish gain, regardless of who it harms.

Both are a form of internalized patriarchy,* the latter clearly a weaponized version of patriarchy that earned it the label of *carrying water for the patriarchy*.

Those who carry water for the patriarchy will be willing participants in protecting the very system in which they are oppressed. Sometimes they do this because they have reached a point high enough within the patriarchal structure that they want to protect themselves by proving their loyalty to the male leadership.

Defenders of patriarchy from oppressed sectors is found in all aspects of patriarchal structures. From the mother who chastises her daughter for not being ladylike because she simply wants to play basketball with her male friends, to the pastor's wife who teaches a class on being a subservient and godly woman, white women have become especially adept at carrying this proverbial water. She may bristle at being labeled a Karen, but the internet is forever, and videos don't lie.

These are the women who take their role to protect the patriarchy very seriously. They do so through their self-appointed position as the gatekeepers of heteronormative standards. The most outrageous are filmed daily, as we have discussed. However, it is the subtler microaggressions that inflict some of the most severe damage to the historically oppressed.

For example:

Toward Women

"Does your family suffer because you work?"

"You're pretty strong for a girl."

"Are you sure you can handle that job while taking care of your family?"

Toward Black People

"You're so articulate."

"Where are you *really* from?"

Toward Members of the LGBTQIA+ Community

"So, who's the man in the relationship?"

"You don't look gay."

Admittedly, microaggressions are tricky because they are not used exclusively by those who have internalized their patriarchy. Even those who are actively deconstructing can be reckless with their words without realizing that they are holding on to indoctrinations that marginalized individuals will find offensive and harmful.

Yet in the mouths of the individual who has weaponized that patriarchy, the microaggressions are intentionally calculated to imply a moral or spiritual superiority. This is an intentional tactic of patriarchy because patriarchy must seize every opportunity to wield its power to keep its adherents submissive and obedient to its teachings.

Even more brazen and not so subtle are the statements that draw a line in the sand between those in power and those who need to be reminded that they are lower on the patriarchal hierarchy. Statements that begin with "I don't have a problem with [insert the individual or group of individuals here]" and continue with a "but" almost are always about gatekeeping* the heteronormative standards mandated by any given patriarchal structure.

"Well, I don't have a problem with Black people, but why do they have to wear their jeans so far below their waist?"

"I don't care if Hispanics live in my neighborhood, but they should speak English."

"Oh, I am not offended by gay people, but why do they have to show public displays of affection? I just don't need to see that." These kinds of statements intentionally imply an explicit assertion of power and then offer a concession as if they alone are the keeper of both.

It isn't just white women who internalize their patriarchy. Candace Owens, a Black American conservative political commentator, is, to me, an example of an individual who is carrying water for the patriarchy to protect her place within that structure. Owens is an outspoken critic of Black Lives Matter and believes that systemic racism does not exist. She has made comments downplaying the historical struggles of Black people that many critics find harmful and insensitive to the Black community.

Another person who I believe is carrying water for the patriarchy is Caitlyn Jenner, a prominent transgender woman who is a retired Olympic decathlete. Jenner was celebrated when she first came out as transgender in 2015. However, over the past several years, Jenner has become closely aligned with conservative Republicans who have supported legislation that severely limits the rights of LGBTQIA+ humans. She also has verbally attacked other influential transgender social media creators, further displaying a huge disconnect between the privilege she enjoys with her proximity to power versus others who are not world-class athletes or who are not connected to high-profile politicians.

Examining how you may benefit from or continue to perpetuate patriarchy is a critical step in deconstructing from your religious heritage. It's so important in the deconstructing process that it is the number one topic for my social media content. The reason I consider it of such importance is because patriarchal indoctrination sneaks up on you. When you least expect it, it'll blindside you in ways that are humbling and revealing.

Humbling because without doing the work of deconstructing from it, you risk being called out when it shows up in your life. Revealing because your response to being called out will expose the places where you are rejecting or acknowledging there is an indoctrinated belief onto which you are holding.

For example, when Queen Elizabeth II died in 2022, there were many people who made videos expressing outrage for a monarchical system* that was a rigid class structure* that many view as outdated and unfair. Given the monarchy's lengthy history of colonialism,* involvement in the transatlantic slave trade, cultural suppression, and atrocities related to human suffering, those making the videos refused to mourn her passing and instead called for radical changes to the structure of the monarchy to more accurately reflect changing culture and values.

Some people were offended by those videos and what they perceived as a "lack of caring" toward the queen's passing and pushed back by making videos to admonish those who made the videos critical of the British monarchy.

The back-and-forth became heated, prompting many, including me, to make response videos asking creators who were supportive of the monarchy to reconsider their intent in making their response videos. Many of them responded that they were only doing the right thing because honoring the dead should be handled with reverence and care.

That is a valid point, but there was more at work here than just being upset at someone's apparent lack of respect for the dead.

What was playing out in real time was the outward expression of internalized patriarchy by those indoctrinated into that system. While it may seem commendable and even compassionate to demand a level of respect and honor surrounding how the passing of a world-renowned statesperson should be honored, insisting that others follow our set of morals and beliefs is a type of gatekeeping that is often used in patriarchal structures. If those in power can mandate the language used surrounding dissent, the type of respect shown to those who have died, and enforce codes of etiquette surrounding clothing styles and "appropriate" conduct in public, this power structure is then reaffirmed.

Let's take a deeper dive into the situation specific to Queen Elizabeth. Romanticizing monarchies is part of our cultural norm that also adds mystique and fantasy to the roles that royals play in our society. Monarchical systems, like patriarchy, rely heavily on a structure that reinforces their above-human status and elevates them to a Divine-like role in society. America's fascination with the British monarchy extends further back than just the late Princess Diana and most likely has links to our past connection to British history. In other words, our ancestral lineage is deeply rooted in many different patriarchal structures, which no doubt spirals up to our lives today and impacts how we view the world.

Scenarios like my coffee shop experience, the mansplaining I witnessed inside progressive churches, and my experience inside high-control evangelical churches play out across America each day. Patriarchy is interwoven into our lives in so many ways that we do not recognize how it is impacting us. Our indoctrination into patriarchal constructs is such that we simply see it as a by-product of our societal interactions and expectations.

It is patriarchy that taught those of us from the silent (1928–1945) and boomer (1946–1964) generations to be seen and not heard as children, to respect our elders, even when they were clearly wrong or, even worse, abusive. Regardless of where we were, a white man could stop us, demand we answer his questions about what we were doing, and we would be expected to answer.

It is patriarchy that enforces gender roles in family dynamics, in church roles and leadership, in positions of authority and governmental control.

It is patriarchy that perpetuates the belief that women are

inferior and that historically marginalized humans benefit from the patriarchal structure.

It is patriarchy that repeatedly has renegotiated with the Bible to emphasize male leadership and reinforce the notion that men are better equipped as church leaders.

It is patriarchy that continues to have its foot on the neck of the historically oppressed, offering just enough relief in the way of rights and opportunities to appear to be progressive and caring in their attempt to remain in power.

And it is patriarchy that has negatively impacted humans, including men, throughout history.

But things are changing, and they're changing quickly.

Many boomers are awakening to the harm that their patriarchal indoctrinations caused, and later generations are rejecting its toxicity with a passion.

Enter the Millennial: The Rejection of Patriarchy

There is great strain on the patriarchal systems in this country. Younger generations are pushing back on them, demanding change and accountability for how they have treated its citizens, its family members, its students, and, yes, its congregants. People today are frustrated and tired of the lack of transparency and the blatant distortion of power and wealth that benefit those at the very top of these structures. Disappearing from our society are generations that believed that to be the good citizen and the good Christian meant you were to be silent and compliant.

While those demanding change are primarily rising from younger generations, voices of the past from those who advocated for human rights echo up to us today.

From the silent generationers like Bishop John Shelby Spong, Gloria Steinem, Archbishop Desmond Tutu, Angela Davis, Harvey Milk, John Lewis, and Rev. Dr. Martin Luther King Jr.

From the boomer generation are people like bell hooks, Barack Obama, and Cornel West.

Even the greatest generation had their heroes of social justice in people like Nelson Mandela, Rosa Parks, Dorothy Day, and Dietrich Bonhoeffer.

All these amazing humans and many more stood in the gap between the privileged and the oppressed to impact change when the vast majority of those around them seethed with rage at the thought of granting equal rights to the historically oppressed.

They are the giants upon whose shoulders we now stand and whose legacy will be that they were unafraid to use their voices to impact change. I encourage you to spend time researching these amazing people and consider what they have to teach you on your deconstructing journey.

That is energy that permeates into each Generation Xer, millennial, and Generation Zer who is doubling down on the call for massive disruptions in policy and priorities in this country, including inside the church. It will no longer be tolerated that both country and church only have the interests of the white Christian man as their focus. Extensive change is required, or the government structure will crumble and the church will not survive. The former is feeling the pressure, and the latter is witnessing the falling away as people tired of the hypocrisy continue to leave in droves.

The dismantling of patriarchy is well on its way. The people who are carrying the pain of their ancestors and those who see the pain on the faces of the historically oppressed will no longer be silent.

When people demanded that Queen Elizabeth's passing be marked with reverence and honor, many people felt that those demanding this ignored the generations of people who cried out for their own ancestors to be remembered with reverence and honor. This is the most toxic side of patriarchy—the side where those in power feel entitled by their proximity to power to insist that societal behavior will only look one way.

The willingness to accept silent submission to white male patriarchy is rapidly deteriorating. Millennials, those born roughly between 1980 and 1994, are often blamed for this shift. However, the data would suggest that a rejection of religious patriarchy was occurring prior to the arrival of millennials.

There has been a steady eight-decade decline in church attendance, and that trend doesn't seem to be changing any time soon.[5,6] The reasons that people give for leaving church range from disenchantment with religion to frustration with church authority. Church leaders continue to double down regarding this issue of why people are leaving church, insisting that those of us leaving do so because we "never had faith to begin with."

This deflection from the real reasons people are leaving church is yet another attempt by church leaders to continue the reign of power given to them by this religious patriarchal structure. It is easy to see why they are resistant to that structure change. Megachurches* and powerful denominations have raked in millions of dollars from church members. That continuous flow of funds is contingent upon people in the pews, and what better way to keep them in the pews than through a power structure that implies church leaders are the closest thing on earth to God's chosen ones?

Denying their authority is equated to denying God.

Who wants that on their conscience, or even worse, who wants that risking their salvation? Not any good Christian, right? Wrong.

In spite of this pressure that church leaders place on congregrants, people continue to reject this ideology and continue to leave church, especially younger generations.

Patriarchy is unsustainable.

I celebrate its demise.

Beloved,

Demolish. Repair. Restore.
    The work to release internalized patriarchy as well as understanding how patriarchal indoctrinations have influenced you is often the beginning of your healing from it.

Here are some suggestions for integrating this chapter's teaching into your deconstructing journey. Remember: these are merely suggestions. Do none of it, dive into all of it, or choose what feels right for you. Continue to trust that you know what your soul needs for this healing journey.

REFLECTIVE QUESTIONS AND JOURNALING PROMPTS

→ *Reflect on a time when you felt your voice or choices were minimized or disregarded due to gender. How did this experience shape your view of yourself and your place in society?*

→ *Can you identify moments in your life where you have perpetuated patriarchal norms, perhaps even unknowingly? What were the circumstances, and how might you address similar situations differently now?*

→ *Think about the messages regarding gender roles that you received during your upbringing. How have these messages influenced your expectations of yourself and others?*

TIMELINE EXERCISE

→ *Mark significant events, cultural shifts, and personal milestones related to gender and patriarchy. For each event, write down how it impacted your views on gender roles and internalized patriarchy. This visual representation can help you see patterns and moments of change in your own journey, fostering deeper understanding and healing.*

4

Is the Bible Holding Us Hostage?

The Importance of Rethinking Scriptural Interpretation

Who Do You Say That I Am?

When I began to outline the content for this book, I thought long and hard about how I would approach biblical teachings that are, to put it bluntly, problematic.

You know the ones.

The ones that are used to persecute members of the LGBTQIA+ community:

> Do not have sexual relations with a man as one does with a woman; that is detestable. (Leviticus 18:22)

> If a man has sexual relations with a man as one does with a woman, both of them have done what is detestable. They are to be put to death; their blood will be on their own heads. (Leviticus 20:13)

> Because of this, God gave them over to shameful lusts. Even their women exchanged natural sexual relations for unnatural ones. In the same way, the men also abandoned natural relations with women and were inflamed with lust for one another. Men committed shameful acts with other men and received in themselves the due penalty for their error. (Romans 1:26–27)

The ones used to suffocate the rights of women:

> I do not permit a woman to teach or to assume authority over a man; she must be quiet. (1 Timothy 2:12)

> Women should remain silent in the churches. They are not allowed to speak, but must be in submission, as the law says. If they want to inquire about something, they should ask their own husbands at home; for it is disgraceful for a woman to speak in the church. (1 Corinthians 14:34–35)

The one that seems to mandate church attendance:

> Not giving up meeting together, as some are in the habit of doing, but encouraging one another—and all the more as you see the Day approaching. (Hebrews 10:25)

The ones that have been interpreted to say that Jesus is God incarnate:

> In the beginning was the Word, and the Word was with God, and the Word was God. . . . The Word became flesh and made his dwelling among us. We have seen his glory, the glory of the one and only Son, who came from the Father, full of grace and truth. (John 1:1, 14)

> I and the Father are one. (John 10:30)

The ones that are used to prove that hell is a literal place:

> Then he will say to those on his left, "Depart from me, you who are cursed, into the eternal fire prepared for the devil and his angels." (Matthew 25:41)

> Anyone whose name was not found written in the book of life was thrown into the lake of fire. (Revelation 20:15)

Those scriptures.

If your deconstructing journey has any similarities to mine, more than likely verses like these were not only problematic, they might have given you pause.

What if these verses are right?

What if hell is real, and I'm headed there for questioning my faith?

What if Jesus really did rise up on the third day?

What if women shouldn't preach, and I've been reading this woman's book?!

What if . . .

Trust me. I've asked every one of these questions and many more. Fear-based theology (a religious approach that emphasizes Divine punishment, hell, and negative consequences as primary motivators for belief and moral behavior) is a powerful weapon used by fundamentalist, evangelical Christianity to control our emotions and our actions. A lifetime of that indoctrination is hard to deconstruct. Those types of questions arise when we begin to push on the outer edges of that indoctrination and challenge the boundaries it has placed upon us.

Is there any wiggle room for growth? Hardly. Growth outside of that belief system threatens the power structure. That leads to more invasive control tactics to bring us back into compliance.

Moving deeper into the deconstructing process doesn't stop the questions. They will still arrive. It's what we do with them to discover the answers that matter.

I am not a biblical scholar. Nothing about my informal training as a biblical apologist in Sunday school or in my more formal training in college or seminary qualifies me to hold that title.

Although I have spent years reading, studying, and listening to scholars as part of my deconstructing, I've never held myself out to be a scholar. When it comes to scriptural interpretation and historical context, I rely heavily on those who have done the work to become respected scholars, and I credit them for the work that they do.

Biblical scholars, however, vary in their conclusions about scriptural context and interpretation. Scholars like Bart Ehrman, author of *How Jesus Became God: The Exaltation of a Jewish Preacher from Galilee*. Ehrman, a leading New Testament scholar, examines the historical evolution of Jesus from a mortal Jewish preacher to the Divine figure recognized by Christianity. To put it bluntly, this book will rock your evangelical world and beliefs.

On the other side of this spectrum are scholars like evangelical Christian apologist and scholar Dr. William Lane Craig, who has offered critiques of the work of scholars like Bishop John Shelby Spong and Bart Ehrman. Dr. Craig has written extensively in defense of the historical reliability of the New Testament, the resurrection of Jesus, and the existence of God.

Now you can see the problem. Who do you believe?

"Who do you say Jesus is?" Don't you see how challenging that question is to answer?

Is it more appropriate to ask, "Who do you need Jesus to be?"

And as your deconstruction journey continues, does the question become, "Who is Jesus to me now?"

I can tell you that my answers to those questions have changed with time, and I believe they will continue to evolve as I remain open to new understandings of ancient scripture and the historical context that impacted the writers of those scriptures.

Some of those beliefs . . . well, I'm not sure I ever truly believed them. I just learned to not question them, at least not out loud. Did I really believe that Adam lived to be 930 years old like Genesis 5:5 said he did? But poor Abraham only lived to 175 because he was born after the flood, and the explanation was that these life spans were a demonstration of God's sovereignty over humanity. Just accept it, sister Karla, don't question it.

Okay, but Jonah? Did he really get swallowed up by a large fish and live in its belly for three days so that the three days could foreshadow Jesus's three days in the tomb? Yes, sister Karla! The story of Jonah is to remind Christians that there is nothing more important than obedience to God so God will show you mercy instead of allowing sin to swallow you up!

But wait, are we really to believe that Job was a real person, who suffered immensely just to prove that Satan is the adversary that seeks to destroy us? Oh yes, indeed, sister Karla. Even when we don't understand God's ways and why He would allow this profound suffering to a devoted follower of His, we mustn't question the sovereignty and omnipotence of God, or Satan may cause us to suffer as well.

Did Shadrach, Meshach, and Abednego really survive the blazing furnace? Of course they did. Did Daniel survive in a den of hungry lions? You bet. Did the sea really part for Moses? Why yes. Did Jesus really die on the cross and rise from the dead on the third day? How dare you even ask that question!

After years of "our ways are not God's ways"-type answers, the frustration grows to the point that one eventually finds themselves perusing the shelves and sneaking a C. S. Lewis book home to discover the answers on their own. Once the seal of evangelical Christian teachings has been broken and knowledge outside of one's religious heritage has been discovered, it's impossible to un-know and unthinkable to turn away.

The paradigm has shifted, and a new understanding arrives:

- → The ages of people in the Bible then become symbolic, reflecting how writers in biblical times used numbers to signify characteristics and a place of honor for the hero in the story.
- → The story of Jonah and the big fish is viewed as a parable, where the writers were teaching about the dangers of tribal exclusivity and the need to see the humanity in other people.
- → Job becomes a lesson in accepting life's unanswerable questions, understanding that justice often eludes us, but peace can still be found after profound loss and suffering.

I'm stopping here, because as I said earlier, I am not a biblical scholar. Just as in the question we must ask ourselves about Jesus, the same applies to the Bible: What do you need the Bible to be?

Only you can answer that, Beloved.

For me? There was a time when the weaponization of scripture convinced me of my moral and spiritual superiority.

Now? I can honestly say that releasing the infallible, inerrant "Word of God" teachings of my evangelical Christian heritage freed me to explore a deeper understanding of the Bible's writings. I no longer view the Bible through the lens of literal translation. I see it as a collection of stories and books that were written by mystic teachers and storytellers over a span of time. These stories reflect how we humans evolved over time. From a time steeped in nomadic life that was entrenched in tribalism to understanding the benefit of tolerating the existence of other people's beliefs and cultures, the Bible reflects changing values and expanding awareness of our common humanity.

When I look back at how much evangelical Christianity must renegotiate with scripture to defend the infallibility of scripture, I find it utterly amazing that I ever believed this. The Bible was passed down in oral traditions over generations until it was finally written down. Today, we have no original manuscripts, only copies of copies of copies. These copies date centuries after the creation of the original manuscripts. Compound that with scribes who made mistakes in their translations or were coerced to change the manuscripts, it's easy to see how mistakes have been made and how challenging it is to discern what is the authentic and correct translation.

Still, for many of us, our faith demanded that we pledge allegiance to the Bible as the correct Word of God, and we dare not question its authenticity or veracity.

When I was in my covert season of deconstruction—still in church but secretly questioning everything about my religious heritage—I struggled with the word *homosexual* being in the Bible. I knew in my heart that being gay couldn't be the reason people would go to hell. It just didn't make sense. I would read anything I could get my hands on that had to do with what Christians believed about being gay, and I always came away defeated and frustrated by those teachings. There was no mistaking these teachings or these verses: Christianity believed that being gay was a sin, and unless someone from the LGBTQIA+ denounced their authenticity, they would go to hell.

Fortunately, I continued in my endeavors to learn as much as I could about these problematic verses that condemned the LGBTQIA+ community. I found my answers in the writings of Bishop John Shelby Spong, who was a passionate advocate for the full inclusion and affirmation of LGBTQIA+ individuals into the church. Spong believed that being LGBTQIA+ was a natural identity and was not a sin or a choice. His teachings challenged Bible passages that were used to condemn homosexuality, and he demonstrated how mistranslations, whether intentional or a mistake, led to the word *homosexual* being introduced into the Bible.

I literally cried tears of joy when I read Bishop Spong's words. He had validated what I had known all along. It made absolutely no sense to me that the Bible would condemn to hell a group of people for simply showing up as who they truly were.

In other words, the answer to the question, "What do I need the Bible to be?" shifted from my no longer needing the Bible to be weaponized to condemn and persecute. I needed the Bible to offer grace and compassion to all of humanity.

But What If You're Wrong?

Contemporary Christian artist Nichole Nordeman has a song titled "What If." At a concert many years ago, I heard Nichole sing this song, offering the conversation that inspired her to write it prior to her singing it. She shared that she had recently had a conversation with someone who was an atheist and didn't believe in the teachings of Christianity, prompting her to ask him, "But what if you're wrong?" The song is a lovely anthem to her Christian faith.

In our evangelical Christian heritage, that question, "What if you're wrong?" was intended to invoke fear. Being wrong about faith meant that your soul was in danger of eternal damnation. It was the catalyst for keeping many Christians sitting steadfastly in the pews, because if being wrong meant hell, then who wants to take that chance?

If the fear of being wrong kept you bound to these weaponized beliefs far longer than you desired, then releasing these beliefs can be intimidating and downright scary.

Because being wrong means hell.

Still, here you are, Beloved.

Reading these words and contemplating their meaning for your spiritual truth and authenticity. No one else can answer these questions about your faith, Jesus, and the Bible except you.

No one can judge you if fear of being wrong keeps you bound to beliefs that scare you more than they inspire you.

But what if you're wrong about those beliefs?

What if humans fall short of our understanding of who or what God is?

What if the table of humanity was never supposed to be gate-kept by religious extremist thought that compelled its followers to believe in their moral or spiritual superiority?

What if?

I was able to answer those questions and others like it.

My answer to all of them?

If I am wrong, I'd rather be in hell with the oppressed than to be in heaven with the oppressor, because obedience to a religion that believes it is a sin to be gay is not a belief system I wish to be connected to.

I know it is right for me because I have peace about it.

My Spiritual Transformation

In seminary, I began posting on social media, writing about searching for meaning, of making a difference, of finding God in my neighbor, of who my neighbor really was. I hadn't completely surfaced as a deconstructing Christian. I had left the church, but no one knew that I had left it forever. Heck, I didn't even know I had left it forever. My writings were safe. Everyone could find something that resonated with their own faith journeys in my words.

When I first revisited some of those writings, I cringed, embarrassed that I could still see elements of my evangelical faith in the words that revealed that I was still bound to and seeking the favor of a patriarchal, masculinized God. I wrote of suffering the wrath of this angry God, and I winced at how my words must've sounded to someone who was questioning their faith.

As I kept reading my words, I softened my self-condemnation because I saw that I had simply been keeping a diary of my own deconstructing. My words changed as I continued deconstructing, demolishing the foundations that had held me captive to that angry, vindictive, patriarchal God, repairing my heart and soul, which created space for the restoration to come in an expansive spirituality no longer bound by rigid, dogmatic rules.

My transformation occurred right there on social media. As my faith in my evangelical Christian upbringing began to unravel, my family and friends still entrenched in that belief system first became quiet, ignoring my posts and then eventually falling away. Daily, I noticed I lost friends, but with each one lost, a new one requested access to my page. "So-and-so sent me your writing, and I love your words. Can we be friends?" they'd ask.

Even though it was clear I was deconstructing, I steered clear from those questions that answered what I now believed about who or what God is and what I believed about Jesus. Because honestly? I didn't know what I believed.

To this day, I still don't know what I believe, and yet the paradox is that I have immense peace with not knowing. Some may be surprised to hear me say this, but it is the truth. Deconstructing has taught me that not only can the act of deconstructing be a spiritual path, but seeking literal and specific answers to unanswerable questions can be a futile practice.

Somewhere between my belief in a vengeful God in whom I desperately sought favor and my belief now in a Divine mystery that humanity lacks the capacity to fully understand or define . . .

I left behind the need for my spirituality to be approved by Christianity.

This is why I no longer feel the need to hear what Christian apologists or scholars who are defending literal interpretations have to say. I've heard it all. I've lived it. I'm a victim of it. I no longer feel the need to reconcile my spirituality to problematic verses, because those verses are made problematic by a system that needs me to be beholden to it to perpetuate a power structure that only benefits those in power.

It has nothing to do with my salvation or my pleasing God and everything to do with funding.

I no longer need to answer the question, "Who do you say Jesus is?" because Jesus was building a table big enough for humanity outside the constraints of religion. That's all I need to know.

I've made peace with it.

It is well with my soul.

Beloved,

Demolish. Repair. Restore.

One of the most challenging, if not impossible, aspects of deconstructing is reconnecting with the Bible. For some, there is no desire to touch another Bible, let alone reconnect with it. The weaponization of scripture was so severe that they cannot reconcile the harm it caused with the healing journey they are on now. For others, they long to find new meaning and understanding in the Bible and are willing to explore how it may enrich their spirituality.

Still, others may find themselves ebbing and flowing between the two. There is no right answer, and you may discover that your connection to and understanding of the Bible will change with time. Use the following journal prompts to help you unpack what is sometimes called "reading the Bible with a new set of eyes," meaning seeking a connection with scripture that supports you where you are right now.

REFLECTIVE QUESTIONS AND JOURNALING PROMPTS

→ *Reflect on a scripture that you were taught to interpret literally. Write about how this interpretation impacted your view of spirituality, and then consider alternative interpretations that resonate with your current spiritual journey. How do these new interpretations challenge or enhance your understanding?*

→ *Choose a parable or story from the scriptures that you connected with in the past. Journal about the traditional meaning you were taught, and explore the deeper, symbolic meanings that could apply to broader human experiences. How does this shift in perspective enrich the narrative for you now?*

→ *Recall a moment when a scripture seemed to contradict your personal experiences or values. Write about the cognitive dissonance this caused and how you reconcile or sit with this tension today. Can you find a way to draw wisdom from this scripture that aligns with your evolved beliefs?*

TIMELINE EXERCISE

→ *Create a spiritual scripture timeline: On a large piece of paper or a digital document, draw a timeline. Mark the beginning with the point in time when you first learned about scripture in a religious context.*

➡ *Reflect on changing perceptions: Next to each scripture, add notes on how your understanding or feelings toward these verses have changed over time. If there are particular scholars, books, or experiences that have influenced your new understanding, note these as well.*

➡ *Envision the future: At the end of the timeline, leave space for the future. Consider what scriptures you wish to explore more deeply and what guidance or wisdom you hope to gain from them moving forward. How will these future explorations contribute to your ongoing spiritual awakening?*

5

When Church Hurts

Healing Your Trauma and Embracing Your Triggers

A gentle warning: discussing trauma of any kind can be triggering. Create the space you need to consider the writing offered in this chapter. And as always, consider utilizing a strong support system of mentors, spiritual counselors, and trained, licensed therapists to work through any kind of trauma, including religious trauma. Healing is not a race—it's a journey.

I know part of your story that brought you here.

Because I've lived it.

And even if I love who I am today,

The work to heal from religious trauma was hard work,

And I'm still working on elements of that.

I always will.

—Rev Karla, 2018

More than likely, you picked up this book because something inside you is hurting, is asking for light, and is asking to be healed.

If that is you, then let me assure you that you are in the right place.

Perhaps you are thinking that you don't deserve to be here reading this chapter because your church experience just was not that bad, much less severe enough to be labeled traumatic.

What if I told you that part of your religious conditioning—often called *religious indoctrination*—convinced you that those experiences weren't that bad? After all, you survived them, right?

That's what I thought too. When I began my deconstruction journey, I had never considered that I may have experienced religious trauma. I dismissed some of my experiences as not being that big of a deal, shrugging off or nervously laughing to minimize the discomfort that was arising when asked to share my stories. It wasn't until several months into deconstructing that I realized that my shrugging off the experiences was a conditioned response taught to me by church leaders, who were never wrong and who were above reproach. I had experienced rebukes from those church leaders if I dared challenge their authority. I had been taught that mental illness was a sign of spiritual weakness. And I had sat through many sermons where pastors preached that abusers should be forgiven regardless of the offense, which always included full restoration of the relationship. Vengeance was never ours—only God's.

How convenient for a religious system that has been proven in some of its churches to harbor sexual abusers and predators to teach its victims to be silent and submissive and never expect retribution? It was almost too much to fathom—that my religious heritage was utilizing tactics that caused great harm to its victims with zero accountability. How had this impacted me? Had I been spiritually abused, or was my faith just weak for even considering the possibility that my church leaders should be accountable for their actions?

Then I remembered something that helped me unpack how I had experienced religious trauma in my childhood as well as adulthood.

Several years before deconstructing, I had worked with a therapist to address my inner child wounds*—those unresolved emotional traumas or experiences from childhood that impact our adult behavior and well-being. Inner child wound therapy is intense work with its effectiveness largely dependent upon the qualifications of the therapist and the willingness of the patient to explore painful memories from childhood.

Something that the therapist said to me during one of our sessions stuck with me all these years. She said that people who experienced some form of childhood abuse are at a greater risk of becoming victims of abuse as adults, as they can be more easily manipulated and triggered into responses that mimic their responses from childhood. This concept is called *revictimization,** and it is something that arises more often than we are aware. Revictimization is the repeated abuse cycle from one perpetrator or abuser to another, and it can occur when someone has been abused and that abuse has been untreated or unacknowledged.

The realization that my childhood abuse had impacted my experience inside religion was a challenging moment in my deconstruction. I wanted to believe that the work I had done all those years ago had created an impenetrable armor around my being. The truth is that we carry the collective experiences of our lives, both the good and the heartbreaking, with us. Those experiences can indeed impact us, especially when we lack the tools we need to protect ourselves from those who seek to control or harm us.

Counseling and spiritual guidance helped me immensely with targeting and addressing my inner child wounds, but my therapy fell short of providing me with coping mechanisms that would help me when I found myself in situations where someone may harm me or I was in a situation where someone manipulated or controlled me in unhealthy ways.

So I was revictimized, and my past abuse, compounded with the lack of helpful tools to protect myself from this type of behavior, made me the perfect candidate to experience manipulative tactics and spiritual abuse.

What does this mean for you? This information is for you to explore as it relates to you personally. Hopefully, you can see why this healing work often means addressing issues unrelated to your experiences in church.

You don't have to have been abused or traumatized to consider how your past experiences might be preventing you from fully examining all the layers of deconstruction that you may want to consider. Additionally, you truly may not have any trauma to release, but you may have forgotten a moment when your inner courage and wisdom were the moral compass you needed to navigate a challenging situation, be it in the church or not. Tapping into that reservoir of wisdom and courage as you move through this deconstruction process can provide a solid foundation for you to live a spiritually empowered life.

Lastly, understanding the impact religious trauma can have on a person's deconstructing journey can help you be better informed about religious trauma and perhaps allow you to offer kind and loving support to those who may be deconstructing and looking to you for guidance.

In 2015, I began outlining courses that I wanted to teach one day.

I still have those outlines, and one of them was titled "Healing the Hurt That Church Caused You." Back then, I wasn't calling that harm *trauma*, because I too felt that I would be overstating the pain I had experienced. I had assumed that calling my pain *trauma* was minimizing the experiences of others, when in fact both can be true. This type of thinking—that my pain isn't worthy of the space it needs to heal—is an intentional by-product of patriarchal and religious indoctrination, which we will discuss more in later chapters.

Because that indoctrination had taught me that the good Christian must suffer in silence to elevate the body of Christ—meaning the church is far greater than one individual, and we humans must endure our life experiences for the glory of God—I suffered in silence for many years before realizing, then later accepting, that life as a Christian in an evangelical, high-controlled religious setting was not only depressing but was also downright painful and traumatizing.

It was during my deconstruction that I learned that spirituality should never look like the experiences I had in church. So often when I share these stories in my writings or social media, my followers will comment or email me to share how those stories resonate with them, because so many of us share similar painful points with our experiences inside the church.

But these stories do something else—they help you remember.

Often, we suppress some of what has happened to us because we don't want to face the pain, especially when we feel as if it is somehow our fault.

This came home for me recently on a live stream when I was sharing teaching about religious trauma. My daughter shared that she recalled being slapped on the wrist by an elder of the church for reaching for the communion plate as it was passed. She said that she hadn't thought about that experience for years and had forgotten about it.

Except she really hadn't forgotten about it—she had suppressed it. No doubt that experience had impacted her greatly, and I could instantly see how it had taught her there were no guarantees that the adults in her life would keep her safe.

Something about what I discussed during the live stream that day had opened a door for my daughter to feel safe enough to share something that had long been sealed away. This is a testament to the power of another's story to help us unpack our own experiences.

There is another reason for the sharing of our stories.

Unless you have lived the evangelical Christian experience, it is hard to understand. Indeed, it is hard to grasp. That isn't to say that religious trauma isn't a possibility in progressive Christianity or in other religions.

It absolutely is.

But the indoctrination into a sect of Christianity that is primarily based in America and is probably best described as modern-day evangelical Christianity makes our experiences unique. This is why it is important that those of us with this same religious heritage find one another. This unique Christian experience that is the culprit behind our trauma means we understand one another's pain in ways that someone who never experienced it simply cannot.

That is why we need one another.

That is why it is our time to heal.

Understanding Trauma

According to the American Psychological Association, trauma is an emotional response to a terrible event like an accident, physical or sexual assault, or natural disaster. While shock can be the typical response after the event, longer-term reactions include unpredictable emotions, flashbacks, strained relationships, and even physical symptoms like headaches, nausea, and body aches.

Simply put, trauma is anything that is so disruptive to your person that it inhibits your ability to process life experiences, from the simple daily tasks to the more challenging things like grief and sorrow, job changes, relocation, relationship issues, or health issues.

We often don't recognize these disruptive events as having this kind of impact on us because we assume that trauma only happens to someone who has experienced something violent or tragic, such as a massive natural disaster or war.

There are a couple of reasons that this misperception occurred.

Ancient texts show that doctors and medicine healers observed symptoms of soldiers who had returned from battle. These symptoms ranged from flashbacks, nightmares, and dark episodes of depression to such physical symptoms as elevated heart rate, the inability to eat or sleep, and even slurred speech.

In ancient times, these soldiers were thought to be inhabited by demons or ghosts. It would be hundreds of years before science and medicine offered an official diagnosis of PTSD*—post-traumatic stress disorder—for these symptoms.

But even during the Civil War, the doctors diagnosed the soldiers who displayed these symptoms with "the soldier's heart," because it wasn't just these symptoms, it was also the changes in their cardiovascular systems—their blood pressure, their pulse rate, even how their heartbeat would be different.

Other doctors would diagnose their patients as having shell shock. You can see that we have known for centuries that trauma is real and extends far beyond our emotional well-being. It impacts us on multiple levels, compromising quality of life and sadly shortening the life spans of many people who experience trauma.

Finally, in 1980, PTSD became an official diagnosis, and we were hearing all about it. We now had a name and a medical diagnosis for soldiers who came home and attempted to pick up with their lives before experiencing the trauma of war. For veterans of war, this was life-changing.

Why did it take so long to finally get a clinical diagnosis of PTSD?

Would you be surprised to hear that this is a place where toxic masculinity and patriarchy intersect with the human condition?

Throughout this book, I will use *men* and *women* as meaning those who were born with genitalia specific to those genders and are living with this gender assignment. I'm doing this to reflect history and how this information has been studied and in no way is intended to imply that I reject gender-neutral language.

On the contrary, I welcome the entire rainbow of people to this massive, expansive table of humanity.

Understanding how patriarchy influenced the well-being of humans is foundational to understanding why you most likely endured religious trauma for years before you finally decided to address it through deconstruction, therapy, or both.

Throughout history, women have always been seen as weaker in physical strength but also in emotional and mental capacity.

Research indicates that veterans who try to conform to conventional masculine traits, such as dominance, assertiveness, aggression, and self-sufficiency, without seeking emotional reassurance might be more prone to developing PTSD. Not only are their PTSD symptoms potentially intenser, but they also might be less inclined to pursue treatment for them. Further research highlights that even men who haven't been exposed to war scenarios can still experience negative consequences and trauma-related symptoms due to harmful masculine beliefs.

Now why is this important?

We are starting to draw a line from familial and religious indoctrinations and this perception that people who are born male are inherently the stronger gender, and therefore, they must suppress certain emotions and be willing to withstand a greater degree of stress.

This toxic masculinity that is pervasive in American culture also demands a blind allegiance to God, to country, and to the values set forth by the patriarchy. This God/country mantra compounded with toxic masculinity created a recipe for a culture that has reverberated for decades and has trickled into our homelives, our educational system, and our churches.

It also sadly has led to a high rate of suicide for soldiers who do not receive a diagnosis for and treatment of their PTSD. Lack of treatment for mental health also contributes to suicide rates in the general population.

This is why this chapter is so important. But it's also why I caution that if you have experienced any form of trauma, this book is a good place to start, but it is not enough. When I was in the hardest, most challenging moments of healing from my religious trauma, I was lovingly supported by family, mentors, spiritual healers, therapists, and physicians when medication was required. I encourage you to look at how you can build a support system that can help you on your healing journey.

You may still not be convinced that speaking about the toxic experiences you had inside church elevate to the label of trauma. But I want you to pause for a moment and consider an event in your life, and it doesn't have to be related necessarily to religious trauma, just any event . . .

That changed you.

That shook you to your core.

That you knew after that moment you'd never be the same.

Statistics show that 70 percent of people will have endured some level of trauma by the time they are adults.

Seventy percent.

So as hard as it may be for you to reflect upon, if you have never considered how trauma has impacted your life, it is important to do so now. This may make it easier for you to recognize and define the trauma that you experienced in the church as such.

Before we move on to speak about issues specifically related to religious trauma, spiritual abuse, manipulation, and gaslighting, I want to speak about CPTSD*—complex post-traumatic stress disorder—because this is the cornerstone to understanding religious trauma.

CPTSD is defined as PTSD, or a trauma-inducing event, that is repeated for months, even years. This is sometimes referred to as *complex trauma.*

I think you can see where I'm going with this.

Beautiful souls, not only is it likely that your trauma is real, but it is also likely that because of its repeated events in your life . . .

Be it abuse in your childhood . . .

Or in relationships . . .

Or in the church . . .

You may be experiencing CPTSD. Of course, this must be diagnosed by a licensed professional, but many of us are desperately trying to figure out what is wrong with us when what is wrong with us is right there at our dinner tables or in our church pews.

Understanding Religious Trauma

As recently as just a few years ago, research has yet to completely define what religious trauma is. Like CPTSD, which doesn't have a specified diagnosis in the *Diagnostic and Statistical Manual of Mental Disorders*, fifth edition (*DSM-5*). Religious trauma is not an actual diagnosis. That doesn't mean it doesn't exist. It just isn't a diagnosis—yet. Also keep in mind how long we humans have been aware of PTSD before it became a diagnosis. Many trauma-informed therapists are becoming more knowledgeable about religious trauma to address the growing demand for this therapy treatment.

Religious trauma has been defined in many ways, and that will continue to be so until it has received an official clinical diagnosis in the *DSM-5*. The best definition that I ascribe to is: a person's religious experience that is toxic, abusive, manipulative, degrading, and even dangerous to their mental, physical, emotional, and spiritual well-being.

Remember the story I shared about my daughter being physically assaulted when innocently reaching for the communion plate? That is a singular event that led to trauma for her that she is currently unpacking, and this story isn't about opening a debate about how to correct a child.

I will tell you where I fall on this discussion, however. Only people who are indoctrinated into a harmful ideology would ever feel that slapping someone else's child for reaching for a communion plate is warranted.

In addition to that, my daughter was sitting beside her grandparents, who said nothing to protect her. What message did that send to her? That her grandparents agreed that a strange old man had the right to violate her in this way, and she was not safe in their presence? When she told me this story, I recall thinking how angry I would have been had I been there.

But the truth is, I don't know that at that time I would have done anything differently from what my in-laws had done. I was a product of that same indoctrination, and I probably would have been fearful of receiving condemnation from church leaders for raising a child who didn't know that grabbing the communion plate was an affront to God.

My daughter is on her own healing journey, and this memory has unlocked some significant things for her that I know will help her understand some aspects of her own life.

Trauma of any kind has long-lasting effects, and religious trauma is no different. More than likely, my daughter had locked that memory away as if she were a bad child, and she wasn't. They were bad Christians who didn't nurture her spirituality in one of the most formative seasons of her life.

Experts agree that religious trauma can be like PTSD and CPTSD. Religious trauma may be like my daughter's experience, or it may look like one of these—and a word of caution, some of these events may be disturbing to you:

The countless times I was told that I had a doubter's mind or spirit of offense because I simply asked questions.

A parent or church leader who admonishes or physically harms a child to "save their soul."

A person being guilted to giving "sacrificially" when they don't have enough funds to put food on the table, because it is what God commands and God will bless them with more money.

An unwed young woman who becomes pregnant being brought in front of the church to confess her sin to the entire congregation before being banished from the only community of support she has.

A pastor who admits to having "an affair" with a congregant who was sixteen at the time, instead of admitting that it was a sexual assault and he forced her into a relationship because of his leadership role.

Telling a child she will go to hell if she doesn't go to church.

Shall I go on?

You get the picture, and sadly, every one of these situations that I mentioned is true. My comment section and inbox are flooded with similar stories, and they're heartbreaking. What I don't have time to share here are the years of torment that these people, including myself, suffered because we somehow were made to feel we were the ones who were flawed. Fear of rejection, isolation, or hell are real threats to the one who has been victimized by those who weaponize religion.

Religious trauma can be a singular event, as I described above, or it can be cumulative over a long period of time. Historically oppressed people, women, people with disabilities, members of the

LGBTQIA+ community, and the Black, Indigenous, and People of Color communities can experience this type of long-term trauma through the systemic sexism, ableism, and homophobic, transphobic, and racist ideologies that are not only prevalent in American culture but can also be found in familial, educational, and even religious ideologies.

For instance, a young girl is told that she can be whatever she wants to be but then is repeatedly chastised and verbally assaulted for trying to live beyond the patriarchal beliefs of her religion that say that women must always be under the authority of male leadership.

A person shares with their pastor that they are experiencing same-sex attraction and is repeatedly told that this type of thinking is a sin, and they need to refrain from that "lifestyle," lest they be banished to hell and, even worse in this lifetime, be asked to leave their church.

A single mother opens her door as she's preparing her children for bed. Standing in the doorway are the elders of her church, who tell her that she is not capable of raising her youngest son, and they demand that she pack his bags, as they will take him to a godly home with a man in the house. And she obeys them and does what they demand of her.

A child is repeatedly told that the reason for his fidgetiness and lack of attention in Sunday school is because the devil is inside him, and he needs to pray harder or he will not be saved one day.

A person is told that the Bible clearly says that white Christian males are ordained to be the ultimate authority of church leadership, and because of this, the color of this person's skin and where they were born will prevent them from ever being in a position of church leadership.

Just like before, these are all true examples. And I personally know each of these victims and have witnessed how this trauma has impacted their lives.

Beloved, religious trauma is real.

It mirrors trauma that is caused by other life-changing events, and it can have long-lasting effects that if left untreated can impact our mental, emotional, physical, and spiritual well-being.

It's also important to understand definitions of spiritual abuse and spiritual gaslighting.* I'm distinguishing between these experiences of spiritual abuse and gaslighting to emphasize their importance on your healing journey.

Spiritual abuse describes the specific experience between the victim and their abuser. This is the relationship where the abuser will attempt to manipulate, coerce, and spiritually bypass the victim so that the victim submits, obeys, returns to silence, or questions their recollection of the events and acquiesces to the perpetrator. You saw this in the example I gave of the pastor who attempted to control the narrative about his relationship with the minor. He called it an "affair."

Had that victim, now in her twenties, not been able to do the work that she had done to heal from her religious and physical trauma, she wouldn't have been able to stand up, walk up to that stage, grab a microphone, and say, "No, we didn't have an affair. You coerced me, you raped me, then you forced me into a relationship with you for years because I was terrified of losing my family and church."

I applaud that woman's courage but am enraged by the members of that church surrounding the pastor to pray with him while just a few people comforted the victim.

There is no greater display of patriarchal indoctrination and toxic religious indoctrination than this.

The basic definition of gaslighting is: manipulation of a person usually over an extended period of time that causes the victim to question the validity of their own thoughts, perception of reality, or memories and typically leads to confusion, loss of confidence and self-esteem, uncertainty of one's emotional or mental stability, and a dependency on the perpetrator.

Understanding what gaslighting is, it is easy to see why this would be a favorite of some religious leaders who become experts at manipulative tactics. If you can make a person believe something other than the truth, you have an unbelievable amount of control over that person.

Spiritual gaslighting is a form of spiritual abuse—spiritual abuse of any kind can lead to religious trauma. In other words, the action itself is defined as one of these and more, such as threats of Divine favor, manipulation of scripture for control of another person, and denial of autonomy and agency over one's own body. You might also hear it called *spiritual trauma*, *spiritual manipulation*, and *spiritual coercion*. Over the years, I've heard terms like these used to describe specific experiences, but it all points to some level of spiritual abuse.

Definitions will get hashed out as a formal diagnosis for religious trauma is finalized. For instance, some therapists are using the phrase *religious trauma syndrome* to describe religious trauma. However, there are therapists who reject the use of the word *syndrome* because they feel the label of syndrome is outdated and can do harm to a victim of religious trauma, as it suggests that a certain subset of symptoms must be present for religious trauma to be diagnosed. We will see how this all plays out over time.

The pastor in the earlier example attempted to use gaslighting on his victim and the entire congregation, a common tactic among church leaders. He knew that rumors had begun to stir, and he tried to get ahead of the story by telling a false narrative and hoping that this would become everyone's reality. After all, he was the man of God, ordained to lead them, and this church had been indoctrinated to not question anything. Obviously, his victim has healed beyond that control. More power to her and others who have been placed in similar situations.

> *"If you're sick, it's because you don't have faith."*
>
> *"If you don't have money, then you didn't pray hard enough."*
>
> *"Your partner left you because you weren't godly enough."*

At the end of this chapter, you too will be invited to consider how you may have experienced spiritual gaslighting in your religious experienced. When I did this exercise, I realized that I experienced gaslighting on numerous occasions.

One evening, I was at church preparing for a big event we were having the upcoming weekend. That was a common occurrence for me. I was a church "administrator"—a label given to those of us who had been assigned administrative responsibilities and oversight for some aspect of the church. There were no scheduled activities on the calendar, although there were a handful of cars in the parking lot. That wasn't uncommon on any given weeknight, with people milling about doing the same kind of thing I was doing.

A car pulled up, and the couple who got out said they had heard good things about our church and would like a tour. I was covered in sweat and dirt because I was tending to the new plants that had been recently planted. Even though I was tired and dirty, I was the good Christian who knew that getting new members in the door was part of each member's responsibility.

As I set out to give them a tour and answer their questions, we had a lovely conversation. They were interested in seeing the children's wing, so I directed them to the children's worship room. There was no sign on the door indicating that it was in use, so I opened the door to find that a recovery support group was being held in there.

Upon seeing that this meeting was going on, I immediately started to back out and escort the couple out as well. The group's leader, a longtime church member, was hurrying toward me. As he got close enough, I whispered, "I'm sorry. I didn't know."

I'm not sure he ever heard my apology, because he began to scream at me, insulting my intelligence, accusing me of being irresponsible and displaying poor judgment for opening the door. The insults just kept pouring from him, and I couldn't get a word in edgewise. I caught the looks on the couple's faces, and their reaction confirmed what I was thinking—this man was behaving unprofessionally, and the offense certainly didn't match what I had done.

Once we were standing outside the door and back in the hall-way, he assured me that the head pastors would hear about my "behavior" and slammed the door in my face. The tears now flowed freely down my face, and I was equally embarrassed and enraged by this experience in front of these two strangers.

I couldn't speak, and the couple just stared at me open-mouthed. I don't blame them. What are you going to say to an experience like that? They smiled weakly and hurried toward their car.

We never saw them at our church again.

The next day, I called the head pastor and asked for a face-to-face meeting. He was able to meet with me that morning, and I explained to him what had happened the night before. I was embarrassed that the tears flowed as I shared the experience, because I knew it would be seen as having no control over my emotions, but I felt it was important to let him know my side of the story.

And his response?

He said, "You seem to be very emotional about this. Could you possibly be misplacing your offense on this person when you're really upset about something else that has nothing to do with this experience?"

I felt like I had just relived the assault again. My face must have showed it, because he set to end the meeting promptly, promising that he'd "research it."

The next Sunday, I encountered the person who had verbally assaulted me, and it was clear that not only was he *not* going to apologize, but he also felt newly empowered over me.

And what of the pastor? He preached a sermon that Sunday on the importance of not being offended and working for the "good of the Lord."

I had gotten my answer. Nothing was going to change.

Yet I stayed and worked even harder, convinced that if I did, I would prove that I was trying to be the good Christian. Still, I found myself replaying the situation, and sometimes I caught myself wondering if perhaps I had been wrong in my response to this experience. How could two grown adults think this was okay, and I was the only one who thought it was wrong?

I must have been the problem, right?

No, I wasn't the problem.

My pastor had gaslighted me.

Soon after, I became aware that something was weakening in my commitment to my faith. This situation revealed to me how disposable I was to church leadership, and compounded with the hundreds of spiritual breadcrumbs that were hinting at my deconstructing, it was time for me to reconsider my commitment to the church.

Not only have I experienced situations like this many times, but I've also heard the stories from hundreds of people who have experienced spiritual gaslighting as well. Even after hearing these stories and describing what spiritual abuse is, there will still be people who may doubt that they have experienced spiritual abuse and religious trauma. Our religious patriarchal indoctrination convinces us that we are not victims of spiritual abuse. This indoctrination is intentional, because if you put yourself first over the needs of the church, then the church loses control over you. Once we spiral out of the indoctrination and begin to heal from it, we then start to see how we suffered under those indoctrinated beliefs.

As with so many other aspects of our lives, it seems we always arrive at a place where we must discuss politics and religion's influence. Here in America, we are experiencing unprecedented times. Tensions are rising around issues of race, religion, and the rights of Americans who have experienced oppression throughout our country's history. While these issues have existed for hundreds of years, the prominent voice of extremist views in government and their affiliation with Christian nationalism* has been the catalyst for much fallout, including 1) those supporting Christian nationalism to double down on their stance that they should be the ruling power in America and 2) people leaving Christianity in droves.[1]

It is highly likely, especially if you are a deconstructing Christian or a member of a historically oppressed or marginalized group of people, that you have been impacted in some way by this political and religious tension. Perhaps Christians' support of extremist political views is the catalyst for your deconstruction. Perhaps you, like so many of us, have had to create hard boundaries around loved ones and friends because of their beliefs that support these views. Perhaps you have had to come face-to-face with your own beliefs and accept that the religion of your heritage is largely responsible for the toxic ideologies gripping our nation at this moment in time.

Finally, perhaps because of your race or gender or sexual authenticity, you have experienced firsthand the systemic racism and brutal prejudices some Americans have for people who do not look like, love like, or believe like they do, or who were not born in America.

Whether your existence is rooted in a system of privilege or oppression based on your skin color or whether you emigrated here from another country, your life experiences will greatly impact how you approach your deconstruction journey. If you grew up believing that only people born in America were superior to others, then your deconstruction journey should include a hard look at how that belief showed up in your life in the past to ensure that it will not be a filter through which you will judge others in the future.

If you grew up facing horrific oppression based on your skin color, your deconstructing journey will look much different. You will most likely encounter deconstructing white people who, although they may be intent on doing the work to be antiracist, can still say and do things that are harmful to you. You will also still be navigating a country filled with white people who refuse to see that their racist and prejudicial views are harmful and un-Christlike.

This chapter can pack an emotional wallop that may have left you unsettled and fragile.

I understand this, Beloved.

Each of these chapters invites you into a deep and sacred introspection of the many layers of your life that brought you to this journey of deconstructing your faith. This book may require you to read a chapter, then set it down for a time while you process some of the sacred wisdom and memories that may be arriving for you.

Remember: your commitment to the work of deconstructing will be more meaningful and impactful if you commit to doing the work intentionally—not quickly.

Healing is not a race—it's a journey.

Beloved,

Demolish. Repair. Restore.

In this chapter, we dove into a sensitive subject that may leave you feeling ungrounded, vulnerable, and wobbly. Assessing how religious trauma may be impacting your life is part of the demolish phase. Here we must take great care in excavating the wound caused by your religious experiences without causing more harm to the vital elements of who we are—our hearts, minds, and souls.

Discussing inner child wounds or any form of trauma may trigger suppressed memories or may amplify the need to address some issues that you have been ignoring. Or perhaps for the first time, you are beginning to understand the link to the heartache that you feel related to your religious experience and why you have struggled to process some of what happened to you in the church.

Take this opportunity to pause and journal about your experiences or what arose for you as you read this chapter. Here are some journal prompts to help you, as well as some action steps.

REFLECTIVE QUESTIONS AND JOURNALING PROMPTS

→ *Consider any traumatic experiences in your life that occurred outside of your religious experience. If it feels right to do so, journal about how those experiences harmed you.*

→ *Consider any traumatic experiences that occurred inside your religious experience. Journal about how those experiences harmed you.*

→ *How have those traumatic experiences changed you? How have they impacted your view of the world? Of the church?*

→ *What steps have you taken or could you take to find helpful coping mechanisms to process those traumatic experiences?*

→ *Understanding abuse and traumatic experiences can help us identify triggers that escalate our feelings of insecurity or fear of not being safe. As an example, as a child, I was tormented by a high school student who lived in our apartment building. He would block doorways, denying me access to my apartment and taunt me by saying I could never get home, I'd never see my parents again, and so on. To this day, I will have a moment of slight panic if someone stands in a doorway to talk to me. Even knowing I'm safe and there is no threat does little to assuage it. I must continually assure myself that I am safe. This is a trigger from a childhood experience. Recognizing these triggers allows us to better understand irrational responses are not irrational—they're your body's way of escalating the need for you to respond to a perceived threat. Writing about what you are experiencing with these triggers may help identify the origins of them. If you already know their source, write about how you may work to respond to those triggers so they are not controlling your behavior to the point that they inhibit you from enjoying your life fully.*

TIMELINE EXERCISE

→ *If you feel it is helpful to add to your timeline, consider marking times when you experienced spiritual abuse. However, because of the sensitive nature of this topic, it is advisable to only do this if it feels safe and helpful to you.*

→ *Remember: this work may require the assistance of supportive loved ones and friends, spiritual counselors or mentors, and licensed medical professionals. Do not struggle alone, Beloved. Seek help to release and begin the healing journey.*

6

Discovering the Divine Feminine

In all the years I was in church, I never heard of her.

Not one sermon. Not one Bible story. Not one teaching.

It was as if she didn't exist or she didn't matter if she did.

But she is here, Beloved. She has always been here.

She has always been in you.

Regardless of gender or sexual identity. The Divine Feminine*
is in each of us.

She influences your life so much more than you know, and it is
time to discover her power and wisdom, for that is what church
leaders fear most. Why? Because they fear that when you come to
embrace the Divine Feminine, you will understand that the Divine
Feminine's presence belongs in the rooms where decisions are being made. Without her, the world is viewed as a conquest to be defeated instead of a creation that should be revered and nurtured.

She is all powerful and all-knowing because the Divine Creator
has blessed her with empathy and compassion. But those who
seek dominion through conflict silence her and create systems that
label her unnecessary, weak, and frivolous.

She is nothing of the sort. She is their counterpart, the other
half of them that balances cries for war with a pause for breath.

She will be silent no more. People are awakening, sensing that
her absence has caused much of the chaos we are experiencing. As

patriarchal systems begin to crumble and those in power scramble to hold on to that power through brutal force and oppressive systems, people are crying out to her. She is the inner voice inside each of them looking for the ones who will rise up and demand, once and for all, a free and just society that annihilates a structure that protects one class of people and suffocates all others.

If your only knowledge of her is through what patriarchy taught you, then everything you think you know about her and how she influences you is based on a lie. This lie is meant to perpetuate the belief that the attributes of the Divine Feminine are not as favorable as patriarchy. You are not weak for expressing sadness and joy through tears. You are not fragile because you care about the rights of others. You are not a snowflake because dehumanizing words offend you.

When you invite the Divine Feminine that is in you to come forth, you are made stronger—for now you are balanced. Whole. Fierce. Awakened. Unwilling to bend a knee to patriarchy simply for the sake of its survival, an allegiance that patriarchy demands.

She has been there all along—patiently waiting, knowing that a time such as this would one day come. Systems that rely on suffocating the rights of others will not last, and people who have been taught to deny her presence within them one day awaken to discover she is exactly what is needed to heal the world.

It is time, Beloved.

Take a deep breath, and in the spaces where conditioned beliefs from our religious heritage once lived inside us, let us accept the presence, the wisdom, the power, the passion, and the ferocity of the Divine Feminine to rise.

I welcome you to discover and embrace your Divine Feminine and forever be changed.

What Is the Divine Feminine?

Please do not skip this chapter. You may be tempted to, certain that all you need to know about the Divine Feminine was captured in that one class you took in Greek mythology. Depending on what was taught to you about the Divine Feminine, your reaction to her name may be one of suspicion, defensiveness, or perhaps dismissiveness. These reactions often arise from the conditioning you received regarding what she is and the wisdom she offers you. Perhaps you read about Persephone, Aphrodite, and Athena. Maybe you have heard of Ishtar, who is sometimes known as Inanna, the goddess of both love and war originating from Babylonian mythology. This is all important information and relevant to understanding the history of how the Divine Feminine was accepted and worshipped. I'll include books in the recommended reading section if you want to take a deep dive into this rich history.

There are many definitions and ways to understand the Divine Feminine. A simple definition may be this: a concept or aspect of spirituality that honors characteristics that are often associated with the feminine—birthing, nurturing, compassion, healing, intuitiveness. Throughout history, there have been goddesses, spiritual beings, and symbolism integrated into cultures and religious traditions that emphasize and honor these feminine qualities.

Inside Christianity, however, the Divine Feminine was overshadowed, prioritizing the masculinity of God to affirm the patriarchal structures upon which Christianity was built. This history in and of itself could be an entire book. For our deconstructing journeys, we will focus on evangelical Christianity's suppression of the Divine Feminine so that you understand how this has most likely impacted you.

For reference, the Divine Masculine represents strength, the protector, the logical-minded, the one who is able to make quick decisions and move into swift action. We will return to this concept later in the chapter. Both the Divine Feminine and the Divine Masculine can also be understood outside the framework of spirituality. But for our purposes here, it is helpful to understand both were integrated into organized religion and then manipulated to control human behavior.

Does God Only Convey the Divine Masculine? Is God a He?

If you were raised in evangelical Christianity, you were taught that God is not only all powerful and all-knowing, you were taught that He is male. It's important to recognize this as part of your religious indoctrination because it may impact how open you are to understanding the Divine Feminine.

This doesn't mean that you have to deconstruct from using male pronouns for God. Perhaps you find comfort in an image of a masculine God whom you see as a father figure or protector of your being. I, however, was eager to deconstruct from this belief to untangle my spirituality from all patriarchal influences.

Out of all the beliefs from which I deconstructed, deconstructing from a masculinized God was the most awkward for me. Referring to God as *He* was second nature. Sentences became clunky, because if God wasn't a He, then how did you refer to . . . *them*?! It just didn't work for me. I continually found myself avoiding these conversations because I didn't know how to verbalize the falling away of this belief in a masculine Creator.

There is a default mindset among many Christians that presume this maleness of God. But to get there—to the place where God is indisputably a "He"—requires an acceptance in English translations that took great liberty in contorting gender-neutral or feminine descriptions into masculine definitions.[1] Some of those translations are reasonable. The Bible was written at a time when men held the power and women and children were seen as property. Still, the Bible is filled with many verses where God is referred to as a mother.[2]

The intent of this chapter is not to continue this exhaustive and nonproductive debate about the gender of God. For many of us who deconstructed, we no longer care about what people believe in God or the pronouns they use to describe God. What is important to us is that we deconstruct from the religious indoctrination that taught us the masculine characteristics of the Divine were of more importance than the feminine.

The teachings that imply that the Divine Feminine attributes are inferior limit our ability to experience the full scope of Divine wisdom. The notion that masculinity is far superior to the qualities of femininity in our humanness has reinforced patriarchal structures for generations. We covered this in chapter 3, but it is important to note here how relegating the Divine Feminine in scripture to a lesser role impacts us today.

But it isn't just the suppression of the Divine Feminine in scripture that harms our spiritual well-being. It is the denial that regardless of our gender or sexual identity, the Divine Feminine—as well as the Divine Masculine—is in every human being.

The Divine Feminine and the Divine Masculine

The concept of both the Divine Feminine as well as the Divine Masculine being a part of who we are regardless of our sexual or gender identity may feel foreign, even off-putting, to you. As noted earlier, this is most likely due to your upbringing that taught you there were only two genders—male and female—with each gender exuding the attributes assigned to that gender role.

But an individual who embraces the spiritual concepts of different but complementary energies of Divine Masculine and Divine Feminine moves closer to spiritual wholeness. Embracing both the masculine and the feminine means understanding that, for instance, crying isn't a characteristic exclusively assigned to the feminine. Likewise, the role of protector isn't one that is exclusively assigned to the masculine. Each person carries within themselves all these characteristics. Learning to balance them and utilize them as they are needed in our lived experiences allows for the full range of human capabilities to be integrated into our lives.

Research confirms that teaching gender expectations based on male and female gender assignments can have a harmful impact on children and adults alike.[3] Telling children they "cry like a girl" or that they are "big babies" can cause the suppression of emotions where the individual learns to disconnect from feelings and characteristics that don't align with societal expectations of their gender. The greater control those in power have over the individuals within that structure, the more rigid the expectations are. For instance, a woman in a high-control, cultlike religious setting where a patriarchal structure places men in positions of leadership will have zero opportunities for leadership within that structure. She also knows that she must submit to that male authority in order to remain in good standing. Likewise, gender expectations would dictate how each gender dresses, behaves, and the like, with no tolerance for gender or sexual identity other than male and female.

These beliefs often get reinforced inside religions where preachers admonish men for not being "the man of the house" or demanding that women "submit to their husbands."

But none of it is true—none of it. Gender expectations reflect societal norms pertaining to roles each individual serves within the framework of that society.

Although evangelical Christianity sought to deny the power and wisdom of the Divine Feminine in order to reinforce the patriarchal religious structure upon which it is built, Jewish mysticism did not. Shekhinah,[4] the feminine aspects of God, is reflected in the teachings of the Kabbalah.[5] This is important because utilizing the same scriptures—the Old Testament to Christians, which is the Hebrew Bible in Judaism—two religions construct an entirely different narrative about the Divine Feminine. It's also important to note that many Christian denominations do embrace aspects of the Divine Feminine while still relying upon a patriarchal structure with men primarily in power. Catholicism, which reveres the Virgin Mary, is a primary example of this. To date, women are not allowed to be in leadership in the church's highest of ordained offices.

The Divine Feminine and Divine Masculine
Residing Within Each of Us

Here is where we come face-to-face with our upbringing and what we believe about the aspects of our own humanity. It's at this point where you may feel elements of your own indoctrination pulling you away from this concept that we are a sacred blend of both masculine and feminine qualities, because to accept this as truth rattles foundational truths upon which your reality is built.

I understand this. I went through this myself. I recall how sometimes I was mocked for wearing my hair short as a child. Even members of my family would "joke" and call me Karl instead of Karla and say they mistook me for a boy. Those experiences taught me early on the importance of gender norms in order to be accepted into my family structure. Compound that with sitting in church and listening to sermons tell me that women couldn't be ministers, it's easy to see how I was conditioned to believe that masculine and feminine could only reside inside the genders to which you are assigned.

Learning about the Divine Feminine felt both exhilarating and scary—another example of the paradox that exists when deconstructing from religious beliefs that create limiting beliefs about yourself. All of a sudden, things made sense. Memories came flooding back. In high school, I stormed into the boys' locker room to confront a bully who had hazed my brother. I was unafraid for my own safety. I was seeing red and ready to fight. I remember seeing the fear in his eyes because he knew I was enraged. If not for the coach who took me aside and told me to calm down intercepting my charge, I don't know what would have happened. After that day, things were awkward between my boyfriends who witnessed my outrage and me. One told me I was wrong. Another told me how I had embarrassed my classmate. Still another told me that girls shouldn't act like that.

No one held the bully accountable for what he did to my brother.

Still, I heard loud and clear that "girls don't act like that." That memory punched me in the gut as I read about how the Divine Feminine is gifted with her unending passion but also her defense of justice. That day in the boys' locker room was the Divine Feminine rising in me. I'm not saying that I would have had a right to physically assault that boy. But I had the right to demand justice, which never came. Instead, I was chastised for an energy that was inherently mine. I was being trained in how to ignore her for the sake of patriarchy.

And what of you, Beloved?

Perhaps you too have memories asking for light. Memories that mirror mine. Maybe you didn't march into a locker room to confront the high school bully. Perhaps you were instructed on how to act, what to wear, how to respond, and what aspects of yourself that you were to deny even existed.

The Divine Feminine and the Divine Masculine have always been a part of us, inviting us to dance as the energy ebbs and flows among our lived experiences. We humans are so much more complex than the narratives through which we have been forced to exist. Whether you identify as male, female, gender fluid, nonbinary, queer, trans, or any amazing color of the vibrant human rainbow,[6] the Divine Masculine and the Divine Feminine swirl deep inside us, inviting us to show up as the complex, emotional, and empathic humans that we are. Denying the presence of the Divine Masculine or the Divine Feminine within us creates an imbalance where frustration, bitterness, fits of outrage, or extreme bouts of depression arrive—and we don't know why.

This is a complex and complicated concept that deserves your consideration. It may feel overwhelming or confusing, especially if your conditioned beliefs were rigid about gender expectations that dictated how you show up in the world.

A Word About Toxic Masculinity

Whenever I teach on the Divine Feminine or the harmful impacts of patriarchy, I will receive comments from people who accuse me of being "antimasculine." Nothing could be further from the truth. These comments reflect an ignorance about the difference between the healthy aspects of masculinity versus the harmful and oppressive tactics utilized by toxic masculinity.

Toxic masculinity refers to cultural norms and behaviors that define masculinity in a harmful, aggressive, and domineering manner. Some of what is common when toxic masculinity is present are

- An emphasis of dominance and control that protects the power structure of men;
- Encouragement of emotional repression and discouragement of the expression of vulnerability;
- Promotion of an unhealthy competitive nature, often at the expense of others; and
- Stigmatizing displays of compassion, empathy, and nurturing as weaknesses.

Contrast this with a healthy display of masculinity, what I call the *Divine Masculine*. There is not only acknowledgment of the benefits of the feminine but a healthy respect and reverence for its presence for a healthy society and individual well-being.

Divine Masculinity

- Represents strength balanced with compassion and empathy
- Values emotional intelligence and the ability to express vulnerability
- Sees power in collaboration and mutual respect, not domination
- Honors and respects the feminine, seeing it as a complementary force

Divine Masculinity celebrates vulnerability as a strength, unlike toxic masculinity, which views it as a weakness.

Discussing the Divine Feminine is not an attack on masculinity. The people offended by or uncomfortable with the rise of the Divine Feminine are the ones who rely on her absence to maintain control or those who do not understand how she impacts their own lives.

Out of everything I offered in this chapter, this is the most important aspect to remember—discussing the Divine Feminine and Divine Masculine helps individuals, especially men, heal from the damaging effects of toxic masculinity.

Celebrate her. Welcome her. Honor her.

She is in you, waiting to help guide you by offering you her wisdom and the qualities that are inherently hers.

Because they are yours by your Divine right.

May the Divine Feminine be the healing balm your soul needs to help you show up as the authentic you.

That is the you the world is waiting for.

Beloved,

Demolish. Repair. Restore.

Inviting the Divine Feminine into our beings is intentionally placed as the final phase of repair in our time together. I placed it here because I feel it is the concept that may require you to consider its complexities and the multitude of ways it impacts your life. Integrating the Divine Feminine can be empowering, especially for those who have felt restricted by patriarchal religious norms.

Spend time with this chapter. Return to it time and again as you feel ready to explore both masculine and feminine energies within yourself, regardless of gender. The balance of the Divine Feminine and Divine Masculine is crucial for personal and spiritual growth. Reflect on the following questions to help integrate this chapter into your spiritual journey.

REFLECTIVE QUESTIONS AND JOURNALING PROMPTS

→ *In what ways do you see the energies of the Divine
   Feminine and Divine Masculine showing up in your
   life?*

→ *In what ways have you suppressed the energies of the
   Divine Feminine or Divine Masculine in your life?*

→ *Have you experienced, witnessed, or even perpetuated
   aspects of toxic masculinity? If so, write about them
   and how those experiences impacted you.*

→ *What steps can you take to embrace both the Divine
   Feminine and Divine Masculine within yourself?
   Where do you sense you are uncomfortable with these
   concepts? How do you feel your life would be changed
   for the better by embracing the Divine Feminine and the
   Divine Masculine?*

TIMELINE EXERCISE

→ *Add moments when gender expectations were forced
   upon you and the impact they had on you (such as what
   it taught you to believe about yourself). Add moments
   when you embraced both the Divine Feminine and
   Divine Masculine. What changed about your life when
   you did?*

7

Reconciliation

The Good Things Found in Church

I was sitting on my front porch early one morning soon after my ordination from seminary in 2017. The sun was just appearing on the horizon, and I had been listening to the cacophony of birdsong as the birds made their way to and from our front yard feeders. This is my version of heaven on earth, and those early-morning sessions are sacred to me. They provide me the space I need to not only prepare for my day but be reminded of who I am. It was the perfect setting as I contemplated becoming an ordained interfaith/ interspiritual minister.

To say I was "deep in the feels" that morning is understating what I was experiencing. My ordination from seminary the previous weekend was still fresh on my mind. I found myself vacillating between peace for what I had accomplished and sadness for my seminary days to be over. As I sat there watching the sunrise and listening to the birds, sadness conquered any feelings of peace, overwhelming me until I was left crying uncontrollably.

Well, this isn't what I expected, I thought. What I had expected that early June morning was to be basking in the satisfaction of my accomplishments. Instead, I was sitting here, sobbing into my hands as waves of sadness continually overtook me.

Sit with what is arriving. I heard it at some point in seminary, and

I quickly realized that I was being invited to employ my seminary training on my first client—me. *What is hurting? What is asking for light? Where does the sadness begin? What is asking for light? What is the heart telling you? What is asking for light? Where does it hurt?*

What is asking for light?

Thankful for the time that morning to give those tears the space they deserved, I sat there and considered each question and then slowly began to repeat, "What is asking for light?"

What is asking for light?

The words began to settle my emotions, and I knew I was moving toward the answer to my question.

What is asking for light?

Opening myself to go deep inside where this wound lay, I became aware that the sadness extended further back than just being sad that my seminary days were over.

What is asking for light?

As I considered this question, I came to realize my sadness wasn't because my seminary experience was over. My sadness was emanating from the bookend that seminary placed on my journey into, through, and finally out of Christianity. Seminary was the end of this story, at least the one that had brought me to this moment, sitting here weeping on my front porch.

The first bookend had been put in place over fifty-five years earlier. That was the bookend, marking where this story began—my first memories of sitting in church beside my grandmother as she sang the old-time gospel hymns in her deep contralto voice. From that moment, I wanted what she had—a deep, immovable faith that permeated every aspect of her life.

For years, I had chased that faith, desperate to be included and accepted by the powerful who controlled my religion. Looking back, I can now see they never wanted the real me. They wanted a watered-down, silent, and obedient version of me. There were times when I was keenly aware of what was being demanded of me, and still, I willingly obeyed, contorting myself to be who they needed me to be.

Now the tears flowed freely as the memories flooded in. The gatherings, vacation Bible schools, summer camps, prayer services, my baptisms (yes, there was more than one), Christmas Eve services, those precious moments with my grandmother, the long hours volunteering, the friendships . . . the community.

The community. That was what the church provided me—a safe space where others who believed as I did came together to build something. After leaving the church, I felt as if I were a spiritual wanderer, lost in the spiritual wilderness—a proverbial desert with no connection to others who were on a similar journey.

When I left the church, I had not only lost my community, I had lost my religious heritage and my identity as an obedient servant, a member of the faithful flock, and a church leader. This type of loss was immense and palpable. For years after leaving the church, I had struggled with losing these elements of my identity. After all, who was I if I wasn't an obedient and contributing member of the "body of Christ"?

After years of struggling in this spiritual wilderness, returning to college to study world religions, and then finally to seminary to become an ordained interfaith/interspiritual minister, I had healed from the harm the church had done. I also found community along the way—in my college classmates, my seminary siblings, and friends I had met in online forums.

Yet there I was, sitting there after one of my life's greatest accomplishments, sobbing as I recounted my life's journey between those two bookends. It was then that I realized what was asking for light.

Sorrow.

Sorrow because seminary was over.

Sorrow that the journey that had brought me to and through deconstructing from my faith had ultimately pointed me away from all that I had ever known.

Sorrow for what I had lost during that deconstructing journey.

Sorrow at the realization that acceptance into my Christian community had always been conditional.

Sorrow that I had wasted so much of my life inside a system that based my value on my submission to and labor for the church proper.

Sorrow that my only choice was to walk away.

They say you know you are healing when you can return to the wound, gently caress the jagged edges of the scar that has formed, look past the events that caused those scars . . .

And remember the good and mourn what was lost.

The good in my religious heritage gave me hope that things would one day get better. The good bound us together as broken vessels deserving of grace. The good meant we had a place where we felt we belonged.

Until one day the good was no longer enough, and then . . .

And then what?

Then one day, you're sitting on your porch crying, realizing that the bookend that ended that part of your life was also the bookend that supported what was to come from that point onward.

That moment on my porch was the beginning of mourning the place where one story ended and celebrating the place where the next one began. The healing parts of me felt safe enough to show up that day to remember the good and grieve what was lost.

On that day, reconciliation arrived, joy met sorrow and blended it with gratitude for what was but is no more, and it was well with my soul.

Reconciliation

Reconciliation—not in the literal sense, Beloved. You may understand it to mean that a coming together with your religious heritage will happen. The truth is that for some, that is the case. After deconstructing, some people find their way back into the spiritual community from their past. That is more of the exception than the norm, but it does happen.

This reconciliation is about opening portals to our pasts to visit the memories where our religious heritage was good. This isn't a mandatory aspect of deconstructing. In fact, nothing on this healing journey is mandatory. But when we reach a point in our healing that the boundary surrounding our lived experiences inside religion begins to soften, then perhaps it will serve you to explore elements of your past that helped develop your spirituality.

We do this type of reconciliation work in other aspects of our lives. Oftentimes, the early days of a painful breakup of a friendship or an intimate relationship require much space to hold the stories of rejection, betrayal, or heartache. As the healing continues, the words begin to soften as you transition from recounting the offense to focusing on your future. The sharp and jagged edges where the pain lived begin to heal. Then one day, you may even feel safe and strong enough to share a memory of a time that was good, and loving, and kind, and gentle.

The truth is that we were committed because it worked—until it didn't. And we stayed bound to our religious heritage because it worked—until it didn't.

Reconciliation invites the memories of what once served your well-being to rise above the painful ones and take its rightful place in your life story. It doesn't require reconnecting with anyone from your past. There is no expectation that you must return to your spiritual community. You aren't even obligated to share with anyone your reconciliation process—it can happen deep inside your heart and soul.

Reconciliation acknowledges the harm church has done while also allowing the good to stand on its own merit. As you continue this chapter, invite your story of what was good to join you.

And when you're ready and if it feels safe enough, reconciliation will arrive.

When Church Gets It Wrong

Sadly, church does get a lot wrong. Would you be reading this book if it didn't get it wrong? We now understand that our religious indoctrination harmed us deep in our beings. We know church got it wrong. We may spend the rest of our lives peeling back the layers of harm and conditioned beliefs to live free from the aftereffects.

For centuries, church has been getting it wrong. In some ways, horrifically wrong. From unspeakable torture inflicted on its victims to public executions, Christianity's history is stained with the blood of victims who came up against the power of the church and paid with their lives.

That description might bring to mind the Crusades, which began in the eleventh century. Notorious for the atrocities committed in the name of Christianity, the Crusades are a tragic reminder of how deadly any organization can become when its power is threatened.

Long before the Crusades' march of terror and murder began, however, violent events in the name of Christianity occurred early in its history. What follows is an abbreviated overview of times throughout history when Christianity got it wrong.

In the fifth century, the Christian church sought to suppress and eliminate sects that it had labeled heretical. The label of heretic, those who held beliefs that were considered unorthodox or contrary to established church doctrine, was a common one used by the church to target a person or group of people who were considered a threat to the power of the church.

Christian mobs were also prevalent within the Roman Empire after Christianity became the dominant religion around the fourth century. These mobs would go on destructive and murderous rampages, destroying pagan temples and killing those living in non-Christian communities.

Between the fourth century and eleventh century, the Crusades occurred. These religious wars are historically significant yet often ignored by mainstream Protestant Christian historians. Even though they occurred prior to the birth of Protestantism in the sixteenth century, some theorize that the Crusades were downplayed by both the Catholic Church and the Protestant churches to distance themselves from their Christian predecessors. The Crusades were sanctioned by the Catholic Church to reclaim Christian lands and protect Christian pilgrims. Their primary objective was to recapture the Holy Land from Muslim rule. In 2001, Pope John Paul II asked for forgiveness for the violence committed in the name of the church during the Crusades.

In the fifteenth century, Catholic monarchs Ferdinand II of Aragon and Isabella I of Castile established the Spanish Inquisition to mandate Catholic orthodoxy in Spain. The Inquisition lasted over 350 years. While historians cannot agree on the number of deaths[1] (ranging from one thousand to hundreds of thousands[2]), it is inarguable that the Spanish Inquisition was responsible for the torture and execution of thousands,[3] primarily Jews and Muslims, after their being found guilty of heresy.

Queen Mary I of England received her nickname "Bloody Mary" posthumously because of her intense persecution of Protestants during her reign. To restore Roman Catholicism in England's post–Protestant Reformation, Mary was responsible for over 280 dissenters being burned at the stake.

Queen Mary's sister, Elizabeth I, a Protestant, whose reign is often referred to as the "Golden Age," began to deconstruct her sister's Catholic mandate by establishing the Anglican Church to heal the divide between Catholicism and Protestantism. However, Elizabeth was not afraid to assert her power through torture and execution to protect her reign. Priests who refused to recognize Elizabeth as the head of the Church of England were executed. By the end of her reign, it is estimated that Queen Elizabeth I, the monarch whose reign is often romanticized as the era of prosperity, was responsible for the execution of hundreds of laypeople and clergy.

The witch hunts and trials occurred around the same time as the

Spanish Inquisition in Europe and the establishment of the American colonies. Thousands of people, primarily women, were accused of witchcraft and executed. The Salem witch trials that occurred in colonial Massachusetts in 1691 are infamously and tragically known for the hysteria they created, resulting in the executions by hanging of fourteen women and five men. More rational minds prevailed when the governor intervened in 1693 to disband the special court assigned to investigate accusations of witchcraft. Struggling to come to terms with the events that led to the deaths of so many innocent people, the colony sought to reconcile with their past by holding a day of fasting in 1706. Five years later, a bill was passed to restore the reputations of those accused as well as offer restitution funds to their families. It would be over 250 years later before the Commonwealth of Massachusetts acknowledged the events surrounding the Salem witch trails by formally apologizing and acknowledging that they should have never been allowed to occur.

The Salem witch trials are a prime example of religious extremism at its finest.

But the reality is that religious extremism was found throughout the world. From religious wars in Europe and colonialism, enslavement and forced conversions throughout Africa and Asia, to residential schools in Canada, native cultures and Black, Indigenous, and People of Color suffered greatly under the progression of Christianity across the globe.

We now come to one of the world's most tragic events that, as hard as it is to digest, is tied directly to Christianity.

The Holocaust.

One of the most disturbing episodes in the annals of Christian history was its association with National Socialism, or Nazism. During the rise of the Third Reich, a faction within German Protestantism called the Deutsche Christen, or German Christians, fervently aligned itself with Nazi principles. It aimed to create a "Reich Church" that promoted an aryanized Christianity that rejected Old Testament teachings. This reinterpretation of the Bible was an attempt to emphasize Jesus's purported Aryan identity and to exclude all humans deemed non-Aryan.

Simultaneously, the Nazi Party sought to remodel Christianity to better align with its anti-Semitic and racial-purity beliefs, an endeavor known as *Positive Christianity*. And the figurehead of this regime? Adolf Hitler, who often portrayed himself as a pro-Christian leader in public. However, behind closed doors, he harbored disdain for Christianity, viewing Positive Christianity merely as a transitional tool. His ultimate vision was the replacement of Christianity with a religion centered on racial purity and Germanic traditions.

The Catholic Church's relationship with Nazism was also complicated and disturbing. The Vatican, aiming to ensure freedom for the Catholic Church in Germany, signed the Reichskonkordat in 1933. This accord required bishops to swear loyalty to the Reich.

Certain Christian circles within Germany drew parallels between their faith and the militarism of the Nazis, dubbing themselves the "storm troopers of Jesus Christ." This militant interpretation called for a combative form of Christianity that fiercely protected German nationalism and racial purity. The roots of such sentiments can be traced back to long-standing anti-Judaic teachings within Christian theology. This connection to these roots provided the Nazis with a convenient platform from which they could expand their hate-filled anti-Semitic policies.

There were, however, voices of resistance emerging inside Christianity. The Confessing Church, a united front against the Deutsche Christen, was born. Among its members was Dietrich Bonhoeffer, a theologian whose legacy of resistance against the Nazi regime is recognized to this day for his courage and bravery. Despite the immense pressure from Hitler and members of his party, many members from the Confessing Church resisted, refusing to sign the pledge of loyalty to the Third Reich. Bonhoeffer notably stood his ground and, tragically, was executed mere days before the war concluded. His profound writings, including the poignant *Letters and Papers from Prison*, bear witness to his unyielding faith and moral fortitude amid oppressive tyranny.

Bonhoeffer's tragic end underscores the devastating consequences faced by those who dared to challenge the Nazi regime.

It's heart-wrenching to confront the reality of how intertwined Christianity was with one of history's most vile regimes. These dark chapters of history challenge believers to critically analyze their faith, understand its historical contexts, and continuously seek ways to prevent the repetition of past atrocities. The church's violent and deadly past is just one way that Christianity got it wrong. That history illustrates Christianity's obsession with retaining power at all costs, then acting universally to threaten, intimidate, even annihilate those who it felt threatened its power. There is no denying that throughout history the church has been a harbor of community and support at one time or another for millions of us, offering solace and meaning. Its ability to keep the faithful anchored to a shared belief and create a sense of belonging has been a lifeline for many. Yet this same power has also played a role in some of humanity's darkest episodes, from religious wars to the persecution of those deemed "different" or "heretical."

This is more than just "collective missteps" or historical footnotes. These are indelible stains on our shared human narrative that underscore the dangers of unchecked religious fanaticism and the "us versus them" mentality.

There is another more intimate and deeply personal way that the church has gotten it wrong, and that is through spiritual abuse, manipulation, gaslighting, and deception.

We call that *religious trauma*.

We have discussed religious trauma, but it's important to emphasize some key points about the personal wounds caused by Christianity that extend beyond the high-control religious ideology found in fundamentalist, evangelical Christianity. As we discussed earlier, many denominations of Christianity, even the ones that are considered more progressive in ideology and belief, are deeply rooted in religious patriarchy.

This religious patriarchy at its core means the church has sometimes been a place of trauma rather than refuge. Spiritual abuse, gaslighting, and manipulation within church can lead to profound emotional and psychological harm, with victims often struggling in silence due to an adherence to church authority—which is often men.

On a personal level, the very place we go to find spiritual comfort—our churches—can sometimes be where we get spiritually wounded. It's like seeking healing from holy water and finding the water poisoned. Manipulation, gaslighting, and outright abuse can happen right in the church pews, masked by the language of "Christian love." These wounds can stick with us, affecting how we see ourselves, the Divine, and the world around us. It is critical to bring these wounds into the light of our awareness and begin the journey to heal from them.

Doing so not only allows us to reclaim our spiritual journeys but also helps our faith communities become what they're meant to be—safe havens of love and spiritual growth.

At least for those who choose to remain in the church.

The rest of us? We find our healing sanctuary elsewhere.

And it is all good, and Holy, and sacred.

When Church Gets It Right

When you are healing from abuse, you don't start that healing by acknowledging the good things about your abuser. It's counterproductive to the healing process. The most important thing is to assure yourself that you are safe and you have a right to heal, then begin taking the steps toward healing at a pace that is comfortable and beneficial for you.

Given that context, depending on where you are on your deconstructing journey or how deep your wounds are that church caused, that statement—when church gets it right—may be triggering. You simply have not reached a point where you are ready to consider the things that organized Christianity has done well.

It's different for everyone, but if this section feels forced and causes you to feel unsafe, simply read on.

Remember, deconstructing is not linear, and it is more common than not to circle back and revisit elements of our deconstructing when we are ready. Your progress is not hindered.

For many of us, however, we do reach a point in our deconstructing when it benefits our journeys to reconcile with the good things that Christianity has done. Beyond the sanctuary it offers for millions of people who find spiritual nourishment within its framework, throughout history, leaders within Christianity have championed justice and love and have advocated for social justice reform and access to higher education.

Religion does indeed get it right quite often, and I'll start by sharing a story of when it got it right in my own life.

In 1979, I graduated high school. I didn't attend my high school graduation because I was nine months pregnant. At seventeen years old, I would soon be giving birth to a very healthy girl. I was a baby literally having a baby. To say I was unprepared for this monumental undertaking of motherhood is putting it mildly. Before discovering I was pregnant at the start of my senior year and just before my seventeenth birthday, I was playing basketball, running track, and being a cheerleader. Life was good for this small-town girl in Indiana. Marriage was not on my radar for my senior year, but within a few short weeks after discovering I was pregnant, I was married to my high school sweetheart.

Later that same year, I would be delivering an eight-pound, eight-ounce baby girl into the world, but not without complications, the details of which are too long and graphic to share here.

What is important to know is that a failed spinal block sent medicine that was intended for the lower half of my body to the base of my skull, resulting in my inability to sit up without excruciating pain that often resulted in my passing out. I was discharged from the hospital in that condition with no answers and no promise for a full recovery.

For seven straight days after returning home, I languished in bed, completely reliant on others for my care. Both my husband and mom worked full-time, so other family, church members, and friends became my and my daughter's caretakers. They arrived each day with food, gifts, and get well cards. Everyone who cared for me knew the drill. Test my tolerance to sit up. If I screamed, immediately put me back down. Up and down, up and down I went several times a day in the middle of our caretakers cleaning, cooking, changing diapers, and doing laundry.

With each passing day, I could see it on the faces of my family and the caretakers—I was not getting better.

I too was becoming very concerned. My feet had not touched the ground for six days. I had not left my bedroom, hadn't bathed, hadn't cared for my daughter, and hadn't been able to sit up for more than three seconds at a time.

I had no idea what my future looked like with this type of injury. How would I ever be a functioning human, let alone care for a child and our little family? Still, I was so preoccupied with avoiding pain that I didn't focus too long on getting better. I just wanted the breakthrough pain to end.

And I wanted to take a real shower.

On the morning of the seventh day, my mother-in-law came for her shift to care for me and my daughter. When she came in with my breakfast, I could tell she had been crying and asked me how I was feeling. I didn't have to ask. I knew her tears were for me. Seeing her in tears shook something inside my immature brain. If the adults were crying about my fate, then I should be especially worried.

When it came time for my mother-in-law to leave toward the end of the day, I expected her to come into my bedroom at any time to tell me she was leaving. Instead, I began to hear cars, lots of cars pulling into our gravel driveway. I listened to the car doors slam, then mumbled conversations began moving toward the front door, where my mother-in-law greeted each person now coming through the door. The conversations now became whispers as they all seemed to be gathering in the living room, pausing to coo at my daughter before returning to their whispered tones.

Whatever was happening, I had a strong suspicion that it had something to do with me.

And I was right. After a few minutes, my mother-in-law came into the room and sat beside me. She told me that the women of the church had come and wanted to pray for me. "Would that be all right?" she asked. I could sense her concern that I would find their presence alarming.

She was right. I did find it alarming. Why would all these women gather at the same time, drive to my home, and now want to come in as a group to pray for me? I had never heard of such a thing, let alone experienced it.

"What do I have to do?" I asked.

"Nothing," she assured.

"Why are they here?" I asked.

"They love you," she said with a half-smile that was intended to show love and hide the concern behind her words.

It didn't work. I was scared, mostly because this type of prayer intervention could only mean one thing—I was very sick.

I nodded, and she quickly rose to leave the room. After a few minutes of more muffled conversations, one of the older women from the church tapped on the bedroom doorframe and said hello. She pushed the door fully open and ushered the women in. One by one, they entered my tiny bedroom, within a few seconds taking up every inch of floor space. I lost count after twelve, overwhelmed by their presence but also the tears shining on some of their faces.

No one said a word. They took their places as if they knew where to stand and whose hand to grab. The room was completely silent until the one who had ushered all of them in began to pray. As she prayed, some of the women began to openly sob. Others affirmed her prayer with "Amen" and "Yes, Jesus." Others began to mutter in words that didn't make sense, as if they were speaking another language. It would be years before I realized that they were speaking in tongues.

I just lay there. I felt comfortable with all this attention and was on the verge of panic that something about me had warranted this prayer session. Fortunately, it lasted just a few more minutes, and they fell silent. Each woman ended this silence by releasing her hands and quietly slipping out of the room. They continued right out the front door, where I could hear their footsteps until they stopped by their cars. Soon, they were all outside, and I heard another round of prayers, amens, and was that singing?

Then the car doors began slamming, and just as abruptly as they had arrived, they all were gone. I was alone in the house with my mother-in-law and daughter. My mother-in-law came back into the room to serve my supper and tell me goodbye. She said she would see me the next day and promised to bathe me in a special soap she had purchased. I thanked her and propped myself on my side to eat my food as best as I could without moving my back.

My mother-in-law wouldn't give me that promised bath the next day. At 6:00 that following morning, I walked out of my bedroom, fully mobile and pain-free.

The dream. My daughter screaming for me is what I remember. It was so real. When I awoke a little before 6:00 that morning, I knew I was alone. Both my husband and mother would have left for work, and there would be a short time between when they left and when my aunt, who was on early-morning duty, arrived. I was drenched in sweat and couldn't recall anything else about the dream except I had to get to my daughter. The feeling that she was in danger felt so real, I didn't know what to do. Without a cell phone (this was the '70s) or landline within reach, my incapacity to help her sent waves of panic through me.

I had no choice. I had to try to get up. I began sobbing openly as I anticipated the pain. Fearing that I would pass out from that pain as I had often done, I decided my first priority would be to make it to the living room, check my daughter's bassinet, grab the phone, and if need be just collapse to the floor with the phone in my hand so I could call someone when I gained consciousness.

Taking one deep breath, I swung my legs off the bed but kept my head and back still. Pausing there to wipe my tears and bracing myself for the pain, I sat up.

The pain was instant. It shot up my back. I screamed.

Then . . . nothing.

I sat there frozen in disbelief. Had I passed out? No, I was fully awake, and I was completely pain-free.

I was too terrified to move. I didn't trust any of this. Where was the pain that had crippled me since giving birth? How was my head not contorting backward in that weird backbend? How was I conscious?

After a few more minutes of sitting on the side of the bed with no pain, I became more confident that the pain was completely gone. I sat there a while longer because now I had another problem—dizziness. Lying down for that long messes with your equilibrium and your strength, as I was quickly discovering. When I finally got the courage to try to stand, I had to grab the dresser. My legs felt wobbly and unsure.

I didn't care. I was standing pain-free for the first time in over ten days.

I made my way to the living room by holding on to any piece of furniture I could grab and clumsily made my way over to my daughter's crib. It was positioned right by the couch, which allowed me to flop down beside her, exhausted by this exertion on muscles that hadn't been used in days. Peeking into her crib for the first time ever, I was taken aback by how beautiful she was. My panic began to subside as I also realized that she was perfectly fine and sleeping soundly.

But that dream had been so real. That dream had been the catalyst for my discovering that not only was the pain gone, I also had full use of my arms, legs, and back, albeit a tad clumsily at that point in my recovery.

I gently picked up my sleeping daughter and sat with her in my arms, which quickly began to shake under the weight of her body. I didn't care. I was out of bed without pain and holding her for the very first time.

I stayed in that position until a few hours later when my aunt came through the front door. She had expected to see the normal scenario of my sleeping daughter in her bassinet and me waiting for breakfast in my bedroom. Instead, she found me holding my daughter on the couch, and the shock registered on her face.

I had recovered from the horrifying experience of my daughter's birth. It would be a few more days before I believed that I was healed. Each time I went to bed, I was afraid I would awake to discover that the pain had returned. Instead, with each day, I became stronger and more mobile and agile.

Medical professionals had sent me home with no care plan and no assurance that I would ever recover. No one had ever seen or even heard of this type of reaction to a spinal block. I was facing a life of complete immobility.

The only thing that changed?

A prayer circle from the women of my church. The ones who had rushed around to facilitate our wedding. The ones who welcomed me into their circle as if I were one of them, even though I was decades younger. The ones who gave me the most delightful baby shower. The ones who dropped what they were doing to combine the power of prayer with the energy of the ancestors to pray around a young girl who was facing a crisis that no one could explain or treat.

Within twelve hours of that prayer circle, I arose from my bed pain-free and walked again.

Who's to say that without the prayers of those women that I would have discovered that I was pain-free on the tenth day of my condition? We'll never know. I've read enough and witnessed first-hand situations that could only be described as miracles. Because of that, I cannot dismiss the possibility that the power of prayer holds some sacred energy that can mystifyingly find its way across this vast landscape of humanity and alight on me, freeing me from what would have been a miserable existence.

In deconstructing my faith, I didn't deconstruct the mystery of miracles—I simply deconstructed from the belief that they only occur inside Christianity. The world is filled with stories much more miraculous than mine, from religious and nonreligious experiences around the world. Whatever this healing Divine energy is, it can be tapped into for the greater good. It is also vastly misunderstood, especially when one group attempts to gatekeep it for their own selfish gain.

I don't have all the answers about what happened that day, but I do know this: One early evening in 1979, a seventeen-year-old new mother, barely an adult herself, received the universal power harnessed by Christian women and expressed through their Christian faith. And she was healed. Had that universal healing been harnessed by Buddhist monks and offered to that young mother, the result would have been the same, for the miracle is available to us all.

On that day, she walked again, and she felt so blessed to have been the recipient of their love because it is a perfect instance of faith exemplified through action.

This is church done right.

The Benefits of Church and Community

Beyond the personal benefits of community in times of personal challenges or celebrations are ways that church—or, more broadly, *religion*—gets it right. In his book *How God Works: The Science Behind the Benefits of Religion*, psychologist David DeSteno explores the benefits of religious practices across cultures. His research for the book shows how rituals, whether from Buddhism, Judaism, or other religions, foster emotional and physical well-being. DeSteno shares that it isn't about a specific religion. Those benefits are seen in all the world's religions.

There are other ways that religion is beneficial to our common good. Below is a summary:

→ Tradition and societal: Being connected to a tradition that has been passed down through the generations provides a sense of belonging that connects the individual to their heritage. This helps invoke a strong sense of belonging.

→ Morals and values: Religion often provides moral guidelines that can foster a compassionate approach to those in need.

→ Neurological benefits: Modern neuroscience has begun to shed light on how religious practices and beliefs might influence brain function. For example, meditation and prayer can affect areas of the brain associated with attention, emotion regulation, and even consciousness. If this study interests you, consider reading *How God Changes Your Brain: Breakthrough Findings from a Leading Neuroscientist* by Andrew Newberg and Mark Robert Waldman. This book explores how spiritual practices, including meditation and prayer, can change the structure and function of the brain.

→ Rituals and discipline: The act of engaging in religious rituals can offer a sense of control and predictability that may help bring calm and order to an otherwise chaotic life. Ritual has also been shown to help people establish predictable patterns in their lives that spill into other parts of their lives in positive ways.

It is also important to point out the role Christianity has played in the development of many institutions and charitable organizations throughout history.[4] Here are a few examples:

Education

Yale University—Founded by Congregationalist ministers in 1701

Harvard University—Established in 1636 by the Massachusetts legislature and named after its first benefactor, John Harvard, who was a Puritan minister

Princeton University—Founded by Presbyterians in 1746

Indiana University—Founded with the help of Presbyterian ministers

Health Care

Hospitals—Many hospitals around the world are founded on Christian principles, including Methodist hospitals, Baptist hospitals, and Catholic hospitals, such as St. Vincent Hospital in Indianapolis, Indiana, and St. Jude Children's Research Hospital, founded by entertainer Danny Thomas, with support from the Catholic Church

Homelessness and Poverty

Salvation Army—Founded in 1865 by William Booth, a Methodist minister

Catholic Charities—One of the largest providers of social services in the US, it offers food, shelter, and support to those in need

Human Rights

Abolition movement—Some Christians played significant roles in the movement to abolish slavery, such as Harriet Beecher Stowe, William Lloyd Garrison, Harriet Tubman, and Frederick Douglass

Civil rights movement—Led by figures like Rev. Dr. Martin Luther King Jr., a Baptist minister who drew upon Christian principles to advocate for racial equality

Science

Gregor Mendel—Considered the father of modern genetics, he was a Roman Catholic and an Augustinian friar who later became the abbot of St. Thomas's Abbey in Brno, Moravia

Georges Lemaître—a Catholic priest who proposed the big bang theory

When You Are Cut Off from a Loving Church Community

Ask anyone who has been a part of a loving church community, and no doubt they would have a similar story to share as my daughter's birth story. Perhaps not in the context of giving birth and the care after but how the people in their church rallied together and showed up to offer the love and support needed to get them through a joyful, challenging, or tragic time in their lives. They celebrated our moments of joy and cried with us in our moments of grief. They showered us with love when new babies came, and they held the space when loved ones died.

They were often the family we didn't have, and if we did have family support, they were an additional layer that softened the edges of life's most challenging experiences. The way they loved us is often why questioning our faith feels like such a violation. Somewhere in our religious conditioning, we learned to equate those relationships as sacred as familial bonds. Breaking those was like breaking a bond with God.

This awareness is often enough to keep people from deconstructing. They simply cannot be the source of disappointment to those who have done so much. It's easier to fake being spiritually content than to risk hurting someone who has offered us love and support when we needed it the most.

Then there are others, like me, who cannot ignore the call to deconstruct. For us, *not* deconstructing feels as sacrilegious as faking it in the church pews to keep the peace. We begin to see that the love and support offered to us is conditional—if we believe what they believe, worship as they worship, and judge the world as they judge it, we're worthy of all the good things that can be found within that community. Step outside of those boundaries and suffer the consequences.

That was an incredibly tough reality and a tougher lesson to learn. As my phone became silent and my calendar cleared, I knew that my worst fears were indeed true. Without my obedience to my church's beliefs and its leadership, I was no longer deemed worthy of that love and support that I had comforted in so many ways throughout my life.

Coming to grips with the fact that church *did* do many things right but also did much to harm me and so many others allowed me to catapult forward on my healing journey. It also invited me into a deeper understanding of duality thinking. Duality thinking, often termed *dualistic thinking*, refers to a mindset that categorizes lived experience into binary opposites, such as good versus evil or right versus wrong. This can be found in high-control belief systems, such as evangelical Christianity. For instance, there is only one way to heaven, one way to understand scripture, one way to worship God, and so on. Dualistic thinking serves those in power by allowing them to set rigid boundaries on what is good or evil, right or wrong, and sin or sacred. The rules are simple: Avoid what we say is bad. Move toward what we say is good.

The remnants of that thinking are challenging to identify in our own lives and even more challenging to deconstruct from. When we are viewing our experiences through a dualistic framework,* if we find wrong or concern with someone or something, we often leave no room for anything good about that person or situation to be possible. It certainly makes life's decisions easy, but it often limits our ability to see the subtleties in any given situation or offer grace to someone whose own lived experience may be impacted by what we are witnessing.

These are good people, and their religious conditioning weaponizes that goodness when we don't live our lives as they think we should.

Both are true, which is why we miss them, *and* we release them with love.

When Church Gets It Right, and We Still Leave

Throughout history, organized religion has had moments where it shines brightly and others where it has left a dark stain on humanity. Christianity is no exception. As hard as it is to read the sordid history of our religious heritage, it is an important aspect for those of us who are coming to grips with the reality that Christianity is not the sanitized, sanctimonious, holier-than-thou religion of the people specifically chosen by God to inherit His kingdom and live with Him forever.

When taken in context of the entirety of world religions and spiritual traditions, it seems a little outrageous if not fanatical to claim Christianity as the one "truth" for all of humanity. Still, for many of us, this religion called Christianity served us well, from nurturing us when we were at our lowest and needed a miracle, to providing the loving touch points in important markers in our lives that reminded us that we mattered to someone.

The good that church did may not have been able to outweigh the wrong, or perhaps you simply didn't care and just knew there was something off with your spirituality that required you to disconnect and find the answers elsewhere. Whatever the reason, many things can be true.

Church was good until it wasn't.

Church is still good, just not for all.

Church has caused irreparable harm.

When our inner knowing signals to us that something is off with our spiritual truth, it's crucial that we be open and willing to examine all the parts of our faith: the good, the bad, the messy, the sacred, the ugly, and the Holy. Then and only then can we heal what harmed us so that what remains are the sacred moments from our past that pointed us to where we are in this moment.

That is reconciliation.

Beloved,

Demolish. Repair. Restore.

Reconciliation is part of the restoration phase of deconstructing. Here we are beginning to rebuild bridges to our past that we can safely cross without risking additional injury from those who have harmed us.

Reconciliation may occur in massive movement, or you may do it in phases. There is no right or wrong way.

*It's all about where you are on your healing journey and
how—or even if—reconciliation serves your highest good.*

*Here are some journaling prompts that may help you
process this chapter.*

REFLECTIVE QUESTIONS AND JOURNALING PROMPTS

→ *Think back to your time within the religious
community. What are some positive experiences or
teachings that you recall? Write about how these
moments made you feel and the impact they had on
your personal growth or understanding of the world.*

→ *Which values or lessons from your religious heritage
still resonate with you? Journal about how these values
have shaped your life and how you might continue to
integrate them into your current spiritual practice.*

→ *Imagine a perfect balance between your past religious
heritage and your current spiritual beliefs. What does
this harmonized path look like? Describe how it feels
to walk this path and how it differs from your previous
religious experiences.*

TIMELINE EXERCISE

*This timeline exercise is an opportunity to plan ahead.
Consider dates in the future where you may want to revisit
your religious heritage and what that might look like. For
instance, would you feel comfortable listening to worship
music that was once meaningful? Make a list of that music
and consider how it might help you to reconnect with that
music. Or perhaps what date you would consider reading
the Bible.*

8

What Am I Going to Do About Jesus?

There was no denying it now—I was leaving church.

That phrase ran through my head as I sat in my car after Sunday service.

Except this wasn't the parking lot of *my* church.

The one where I could no longer deny that I was in a crisis of faith, and the church environment was exacerbating it.

The one where I was told I had a spirit of offense.

The one where they would gaslight its members into believing that our free labor was intricately tied to our worthiness as a good Christian.

The one where they believed that the LGBTQIA+ community was going to hell but hid those beliefs behind the rock band and pastors in jeans onstage so they could grow into the next greatest megachurch.

The one where I finally saw through the façade of my church's structure. From the counterfeit piety to the spiritual manipulation, I finally understood how this Christian denomination sect relied on the exploitation of people's assets and emotions to perpetuate an institution that hid its finances and the monumental wealth they were accumulating.

All in the name of Jesus.

That church was the one where I had walked out of the doors that Sunday several weeks before, vowing I'd never return.

That church broke me in ways that I wasn't sure were possible to heal.

Before that day, however, I had never considered leaving that church was the beginning of leaving church for good.

Yet here I was, sitting in this church's parking lot, finally realizing that whatever was happening to me was much deeper than just leaving *that* church—*my* church.

I was leaving *the* church, and it felt like I was leaving it forever.

If There Was a Hell, I Was Going to It

Given that I had spent an entire lifetime devoted to evangelical Christianity, it shouldn't be surprising that when I walked out of my church that I was still holding on to the indoctrinated beliefs of my religious heritage—that is, at least the ones that reflected who I believed I was and what I believed salvation was. I left church believing that

→ I was a sinner for not obeying church authority.
→ I may risk going to hell if I didn't reconcile with my religious heritage in some way.
→ I was inherently flawed for not being able to come under the obedience of church authority.
→ I needed to quickly reconcile with a spiritual community to lessen the risk that I would be influenced by the secular world.

In other words, I still believed that my crisis of faith was a *Christian* crisis of faith. It never even occurred to me to look at it otherwise. I only knew spirituality through the structure of the Christian religion. Yes, I may have been dipping my toe into seeking answers about spirituality from others that were not connected to my religious heritage, but I had not yet deconstructed from those beliefs.

I was a Christian, and I had left the church but still believed that all I needed was the right church and all would be well.

Except that isn't what happened.

What happened was an exhaustive search of area churches that may have the secret and sacred formula for what I was looking for. I searched websites and listened to sermons to several area churches. I attended several only to discover that many of them were following the same megachurch model that my former church had in hopes of attracting more people by distracting them with spotlights and a rock band. I even drove an hour away (one way) for several Sundays to see if a liberal, community-focused church founded by members of the LGBTQIA+ would resolve this crisis of faith.

None of them would soothe this spiritual crisis.

Not even close.

I was still convinced that church was a requirement for my spiritual well-being. Determined to not give up, I went to one more church in my area that I hadn't tried.

And now, here I was, sitting in the parking lot of this church and finally beginning to accept that this crisis of faith was not going to be resolved by the source of my wounds, my confusion, my experiences of misogyny, gaslighting, and manipulation.

I had reached the end of my relationship with church.

I was officially unchurched and no closer to resolving my crisis of faith.

I continued to sit in my car, contemplating what this new awareness meant for me, my faith, my Christian identity, my resolve. I could literally sense the proverbial crossroads where I was now standing. I also knew it was my choice, and it was a familiar one. I could continue to pretend I was going to find my answers within a religious framework that was crumbling around me, or I could accept the invitation to go deeper into the spiritual wilderness where

I knew nothing about what I would discover or who I'd be once I emerged from this journey.

I already knew the answer to this question. I had just blown up my life as a Christian. That sentence only sounds dramatic to the person who has no experience in deconstructing from a high-control religious belief system. For those of us who have experienced this, they know I'm not exaggerating. The life I had known months before was completely gone, and I was still searching for answers about my spirituality, yet they continued to evade me.

As I continued to sit in my car, staring at the "Welcome! You're loved here!" sign planted in the church's front yard, I was able to finally see that I was searching for those answers in the wrong place.

The answers I was seeking were waiting for me down the path I was now ready to take.

Even as the final vestiges of what remained of my love for my Christian faith screamed at me to not turn away from what had been up to this moment the entirety of my spiritual story, a sense of calm began to wash over me. There it was, once again, that familiar paradox that is found in the spiritual wilderness, where no answers were apparent, no road map given, and no expectations of who I'd become if I wasn't a devoted Christian.

Putting the car in gear and heading down the church's winding driveway, I headed home with one thought—a question—breaking through my resolve, tugging at me like a love story from my past. I would carry that question into the darkness of the spiritual wilderness, where even today I find that it still holds influence over my life.

That question would be the catalyst that would eventually lead me back to elements of my religious heritage that still hold meaning and sacredness to me.

That question connects me to the good things from my childhood—my grandmother, my passion for activism, the stories where people used our faith to elevate the human condition.

I hold on to that question as a reminder that even today my

faith is evolving, because an evolving faith reflects a commitment to live with an awakened soul.

That question is everything to me, but on that day, I struggled with a sense of betrayal for the answers that were trying to rise up and convince me to turn the car around. I had spent a lifetime being taught that there was only one place the true answers to that question could be found, and that was in the church from which I was now driving away.

Still I kept driving, and I'm so grateful that I trusted my inner knowing over the conditioned responses that had been instilled in me since childhood. Because that question belonged to me with or without the Christian framework. I have protected it with a fierce passion and can now state with the utmost confidence that I carry the answers deep within my soul.

On that day, as I drove away from church for the final time, I allowed the question to settle into me, finding comfort in knowing that its presence within me would keep me moving forward until I could one day be able to finally answer . . .

What Am I Going to Do About Jesus?

That question had been a beacon of my faith long before the day I had heard it so distinctly as I drove away the final time from church. It had been guiding me in all the hundreds of hours of volunteer work that I had given my church, and it had been the catalyst for me to seek formalized training in ministry.

I had always had a call to ministry. Sitting in those church pews in my childhood, I had been captivated by the preacher's words. I can see it now. When I heard that little voice inside me say, "I can do that," it was telling me the truth. I could do that with passion, fire, and purpose. Just because the Southern Baptist church wasn't going to allow me to preach didn't mean I *couldn't* preach. Had I figured that out sooner, I wouldn't have wasted so many years exhausting myself trying to scratch that itch to be a minister through volunteering for Bible studies, children's programs, nursery duty, and outreach and events. For a while, all that busyness worked. I was too busy to notice that I wasn't fulfilled, and my spiritual life was slowly dying inside me.

I explained earlier how I still sought the advice of my pastors about formal ministry training even when I was covertly questioning everything about my religious heritage and what I believed. It was at this meeting that he didn't hesitate to inform me all I needed was the church's in-house ministry program.

Wait. Our church had a ministry program? I didn't even know this was a program the church offered. I was skeptical about it and doubtful that this was the kind of program I was looking for.

My response to the pastor's suggestion that I join their in-house ministry program was disappointment. I was now clearly seeing through the façade of church leaders' advice that pointed people back into volunteer service for the church.

That isn't to say that volunteerism inside the church is inherently wrong. But when a pastor says, "God told me to tell you to XYZ," and that XYZ leads to doing something unpaid for the church, that is one of the most toxic forms of spiritual manipulation. This type of manipulation was rampant at this church, and I had comforted several people who were exhausted by their workload yet too afraid to say anything, for fear of rejection or retribution by church leaders.

I suspected that this in-house ministry program was more about training volunteers to be even more committed to unpaid labor by binding ministry training with essential job assignments and calling it "the Lord's work." I would soon find out that my suspicions were correct, but not before I signed up and became a member of that year's ministry-in-training cohorts.

I joined the ministry program after paying the fee and attending an orientation session. Our instructors were the ministers, other church leaders, and Bible study teachers who were in college for course studies not related to religion. The program was part Bible study, part "activation of the gifts of the Holy Spirit," with a spattering of required books that reinforced the literal interpretation of the Bible. Each week, we were to have a "counseling session" with one of the program's leaders. Mine was a twenty-one-year-old undergraduate whose job it was to review my journal reflections and provide feedback on my spiritual well-being. It was as awkward as you can imagine it was. Here I was, a woman approaching fifty years of age, being counseled by someone half my age and with no training in spiritual counseling or seminary preparation.

Still, I remained committed to seeing this program through to its completion. I was eager to be ordained and wanted an avenue to use my gifts of intuitive knowing and insight to help others. Even though I was disillusioned by the lack of experience of the staff and the absence of academic studies, I vowed to be enthusiastic and attentive to this program.

As time went on, however, I came to realize that completion of this program did not guarantee ordination. In fact, there was no information within the curriculum that listed the requirements to be ordained. What became clear was that this program was the portal that one must pass that allowed you to be invited into a new level of leadership—all unpaid, of course. Then and only then, and after some unspecified amount of time, the church leaders *may* consider you worthy of becoming ordained into the church's ministry.

In other words, I had just paid for a program to have the privilege to provide additional hours of free labor that may or may not lead to my ordination. To add validation to my growing concern and suspicion about this program, I discovered that although dozens of people had gone through this ministry preparation course within the past few years, only two people had been ordained.

Two.

The odds were stacked against me. Yet here I was, meeting with my twenty-one-year-old "spiritual counselor," who had zero training outside of what the church had provided but was now being charged with the heavy responsibility of shepherding an entire class of ministry hopefuls through the program. I dutifully memorized verses, wrote sermons that I knew I would never be asked to deliver at this church, and worked additional countless hours for a church that saw me as nothing more than a commodity to be used instead of a qualified person to be uplifted and encouraged.

Regardless of my commitment to this program, I would not finish it.

I would leave the church for good and with it the dreams of becoming an ordained minister.

Or so I thought.

Your Calling Is Not Exclusive to Christianity

People will often ask me about the words or phrases I use that are considered Christian-centric. Throughout my deconstruction, my use and understanding of many of those words and phrases have changed. As an example, because I have deconstructed from salvation theology, I would only use that phrase to explain how this belief distracted me from being an agent of change to ease the world's suffering.

Same with redemption. I no longer believe in Jesus's crucifixion as a necessary part of the Jesus narrative and invite my followers into a new understanding about redemption as it reflects to everyday lived experiences.

When I speak about prayer, which I still may engage in as a part of my spiritual practices, I'm not speaking about praying to a patriarchal God that will zap my desires into existence. Prayer to me now means connecting this indwelling presence, which is my soul or spirit, to the universal Divine mystery and inviting this Holiness into my being.

Faith is not about exclusive allegiance to Christianity. It's about believing that there is something Divine and Holy that exists outside the grip and realm of our human understanding, and I'm committed to moving as close to it as I can, although I don't completely understand it.

Grace is not an actionable deed by God but rather an offering we give to others whose struggles and lived experiences have influenced how they show up in the world.

Sin—well, that could be an entire book in and of itself. Perhaps someday it will be. Plainly stated, sin is contingent upon theological concepts and biblical interpretation, thereby making its definition incredibly subjective and weaponized. Sin for me is anything in my life that prevents me from showing up as the best version of myself. My refusal to release anger and bitterness and my refusal to face repetitive and harmful patterns of behavior are sins. My outward expression of sin is how I treat others.

Worship extends far beyond Sunday mornings. It is a way of life.

God is not the old, gray-haired man sitting in the chair. To make it clear that I no longer believe this, I often ask, "Who or what is God?" That statement makes it obvious that my beliefs have shifted.

As you deconstruct, you too will reexamine what these words mean to you. How do they serve your spiritual journey, and how do you define them outside of your religious heritage indoctrination? Doing so is not shameful or a sin. It is sacred. No religion holds the power to gatekeep words that are universally used to describe a spiritual truth or experience, even if your religious conditioning taught you otherwise.

That brings us to this concept of "your calling." At the beginning of this chapter, I shared my calling to ministry. Given that I am an ordained interfaith/interspiritual minister, it's obvious that my definition of what a calling is has evolved.

In a Christian-centric context, the phrase *your calling* holds a profound significance. It refers to the purpose or mission that a patriarchal God has designated for an individual's life. This calling is seen as Divinely inspired and is not just about a career or profession but rather encompasses a broader understanding of one's role and purpose in the world.

A calling in this context can be very broad. Some examples

are vocational (clergy), spiritual "gifts" (a common label for those who volunteer inside church in unpaid roles), or a spirit quest or journey (like a retreat or pilgrimage of discovery).

A calling is not contingent upon a Christian-centric belief or ideal. It's much more expansive and universal. A calling is a deep-seated sense of purpose or direction in one's life, often believed to be Divinely inspired.

For years, I knew I would serve in ministry, and I contorted myself and forced that calling to fit inside the Christian narrative.

Even when I was in a church that affirmed women, I left when I learned that the patriarchal structure that was in place would never allow me to fully realize the gifts that I knew I had for teaching. I came to realize that patriarchy is patriarchy and that this power structure, regardless of where it was in place, was going to limit what I knew I was being called to do.

So while I was beginning to see the harm that Christianity was causing me, I was also awakening to my calling, and once I accepted that I did have a calling and I was being equipped to bring that into the world, I knew that my calling would never be fully realized inside the church.

In other words, I finally had come to realize that church was the structure that was keeping me from my true authenticity and my spirituality.

So now I offer this to you.

What do you think of when you hear *calling*? You also may consider it through the Christian-centric lens that implies a calling on one's heart to do the Christian God's will.

That isn't what I felt at all.

I simply felt a spiritual nudge to do my part to elevate the human condition, work for the good of the whole, and leave the world a little better because I was here.

That is what a calling is—a spiritual nudge, an inner knowing, a hunch, or a gut feeling.

The way we experience this "indwelling presence," as Father Thomas Keating describes it, and the message we receive from it is as different as the way we describe spirituality or even who or what God is.

I choose to use *calling* because while it is widely known as a Christian experience, it absolutely isn't.

A calling can be described as something as simple as this— move toward the pain in the world that breaks your heart and be a part of the balm that soothes it.

No doubt you have had those experiences where you hear a story, you see a movie, and you become aware of something that immediately brings tears to your eyes or breaks your heart. You can't stop thinking about it, and something inside you says you must do something about it!

But a calling can also be a talent.

Your love of singing, of dancing, of crafting or artistry is a magnificent gift you want to master and offer to the world.

Your calling may not be to go to seminary. But here's why this is important for you, especially those of us who came from high-demand, high-control church experiences.

Inside that structure, unless you were using your talents for God, they were considered "of the world."

Being in the world and not of it is another Christian teaching that in some churches becomes a tactic for control. You may be invited to sing for the church unpaid because that's what God wants you to do.

Meanwhile, all the other staff members at the church are paid, except the work that you are doing has been categorized as un-paid and "just for the Lord's work." People who are crafty are recruited to use their carpentry, woodworking, and painting skills at no charge.

And while giving and donating your time and talent, as they often say, is commendable, if it is preventing you from recognizing your own gifts and amplifying them in ways that help others and are also enriching for you, or even provide revenue for you, that is a lopsided relationship where your sacrifice simply isn't fair. There is absolutely no road to salvation that is paved, because you volunteer your time at church regardless of how it is packaged and marketed by church leaders. Do you do it because you want to help your community? That's fine—not for the work of the Lord.

Following the Calling

When I left the church, my plans to be ordained through my church's ministry program were abandoned. This fell far down the list of things that I was struggling with after leaving the church, barely registering disappointment. It wasn't that I didn't want to be involved in an ordination ministry program. It was that this one had proven to be such a disappointment in its quality and outcome that I was glad to have moved beyond it.

Yet the call to ministry wouldn't leave me. That surprised me, frustrated me even. I was dealing with so much of what one feels when leaving the church and entering the active phase of deconstructing: loneliness mixed with peace, guilt mixed with relief, shame mixed with validation, regret mixed with hope for the future, and anger mixed with clarity.

The last thing I needed was to still hear this "still, small voice" inviting me to explore what ministry opportunities looked like outside of the church.

I recall an episode where I had been on my prayer bench, and while praying, I began to wonder what seminary I would attend. The thought startled me, and I abruptly stood up and ended the prayer session, pausing at the door of my prayer room to look back and declare to God, "I won't come back in here until you start talking sense!"

Yes, I have come a long way in my deconstructing journey because I no longer have those conversations with God. My prayer time is much gentler and more loving.

Except it didn't work. The desire to embrace this calling and dive into studies led me to Indiana Wesleyan University, a Bible-based college with an impressive online learning forum. A year into that program, I realized that Bible studies on an academic level that were based on the literal translation of scripture were not serving me. After one heated exchange, where I revealed too much about how I was questioning the veracity of the Bible and my religious heritage, my fellow classmates advised that I seek biblical counseling before I continued to "stray into the arms of the devil." I ended my education at Indiana Wesleyan and began the search for a new experience. That is where I discovered Arizona State University's religious studies program in religion, culture, and public life. If there was a major university that was ahead of the curve for online learning, it was ASU. Within ten days, I was registered, my credits transferred from my various learning institutions, and I was enrolled in several religious studies courses and a writing course.

By the second week of classes, I came face-to-face with the biggest crisis of faith of my life—I lost the Jesus of my religious heritage.

"What Am I Going to Do About Jesus?" Is Answered

There would be no ignoring this question now.

No longer protected by the boundaries put in place by existential Christian studies that demand that the Bible be seen as infallible, inerrant, and God-breathed and that everything happened just as it was written, I came face-to-face with Jesus. Jesus not as I was taught to believe in Him but as the world sees Him.

Prior to ASU, the question had echoed in my mind for years, but I repeatedly ignored it. I pretended that it would just work itself out with time. I desperately needed it to because it was a question that I didn't want to answer.

But I was wrong.

Instead of the question dissipating with time, it became intenser. Like the pile of laundry ignored in the corner of the clean room, the question reminded me that cleaning up what my religious heritage had done to me meant I couldn't ignore the corners where the hardest work was hiding in plain sight.

I'm not going to lie. It felt more than uncomfortable—it felt intrusive. Why *must* I answer this question? Look around the room of my deconstruction. Gaze upon the work that I had already done to clear out the clutter that Christianity had piled upon me. I had sifted through the indoctrinated beliefs that no longer served my highest good. I had tossed out piles upon piles of sermons that had convinced me that I was a sinful human for merely being born. I had tidied up the emotional baggage left over from my religious trauma, and I had kicked to the curb all the unnecessary thoughts cluttering my mind about who I was if I wasn't what church said I was.

My room of deconstruction was nearly spotless, and I took great pride in the work I had done. I could live with that annoying unanswered question looming in the corner. I had had just enough energy to get this far in my deconstruction, and I rationalized that "no one's perfect, Karla. Just let it be."

Except I couldn't just let it be. My eyes often set upon that corner when I first awoke, especially in the early-morning hours. Those used to be my "time with Jesus" in another phase of my life. Those times didn't exist anymore. In its place were hours of study, quiet contemplation, deep questioning, or simply rest.

There's nothing wrong with what replaced that time with Jesus. I've been at peace with an evolving journey that expanded my spiritual toolbox in which I can reach in and grasp a new ritual or practice that settles my soul.

What was wrong is that the question was inviting me deep into the corner of my deconstruction to come face-to-face with a fundamental aspect of my former faith—the belief in and relationship with Jesus.

It was time to tackle that corner with the dirty laundry. Ignoring it ensured my room would never be as clean as would be necessary for my healing and my spiritual journey to be as enriching as it could be.

It was time to answer the question . . .

"What am I going to do about Jesus?"

A Love Song for a Savior

Buckle up for this one, sister. This may take you down some rabbit holes that you weren't expecting. At least it did me.

This isn't to be exclusionary toward any men reading this, but I do believe this chapter may hit differently for women.

Did we ever really stop and think about the imagery of Jesus that was part of our indoctrination? I hadn't before I committed to dissecting the question, "What am I going to do about Jesus?"

It wasn't an easy question to answer for many reasons. Much more complicated than the question that had arrived early in my deconstruction, "Do you believe in God?"

That one is easy. I no longer believe in the God of my religious heritage. The one who delights in the smell of burning flesh and offers instructions on how to slay children. The one who supposedly intercedes on behalf of my favorite sports teams or when I can't seem to find a convenient parking space. I rarely feel a sense of obligation to explain beyond what I *don't* believe about God. Primarily because it isn't anyone's business. Our spiritual journeys can exist congruently without an interdependence on issues of faith.

At least that is the way it should be.

I could easily approach the question, "What am I going to do about Jesus?" from the same perspective, but in and of itself, it is asking for a *different* kind of answer. One in which I must come face-to-face with an existential part of who I am, and who I am is that little girl who always loved Jesus.

From the beginning of our religious indoctrination, especially in evangelical Christianity, this falling in love with Jesus is intentional. As children, we're encouraged to take those little pieces with the funny-feeling backs and place them on the felt board. From there, we mimic Jesus riding triumphantly on a donkey, or sitting beside a person with leprosy, or laughing with children, or dipping oodles of fish from a basket barely large enough to hold a loaf of bread, or . . .

It's endless. We then are told how Jesus is our father in heaven, always watching over us, always listening to our prayers, always protecting us from Satan. And remember, kids, "Jesus loved you so much that He died for you."

A father who loved me so much that He sent His son to die for me because I, as a six-year-old child, was so full of sin that I needed to be saved from my own deplorableness.

Nothing to see here, folks, except the beginning of religious patriarchal indoctrination, and this one is deep.

The songs we sing further reinforced this belief.

"Yes, Jesus loves me. The Bible tells me so."

"He's got the whole world in His hands."

"Jesus loves the little children of the world."

These teachings that force us into a subservient relationship with Jesus and equate Him as our heavenly father bridge the gap between religious patriarchy and our familial teachings of obedience to our parents and authority figures is an act of service that pleases God.

But it's all good because Jesus loves us, and He loves us just like our parents do. He wants a loving relationship with us. He wants to know us. He wants us to share our hearts and tell Him our deepest secrets. You know—the way you would your best friend.

Now the stage is set for a child who may spend a lifetime existing in servitude to a religious system that convinces them they're nothing without it. A child who continually wrestles with the concept of a Savior who died for them, who is pleased with them when they submit to the "will of the Lord" and obeys without questioning, even though they may have doubts and questions. In a high-control patriarchal religious structure, those questions are rarely voiced, for fear of rejection or judgment.

Children as young as six figure that one out quickly—at least I did.

We enter our teens with these teachings deeply ingrained in us just as we are becoming aware of our maturing bodies. Now the teachings about Jesus subtly shift beyond that of a fatherlike figure to one with whom we can have an intimate relationship. All we must do is trust Him, and He will be there for us like no one else.

Once again, the songs reflect this shift from loving father to intimate partner.

"In the Garden"—a song with lyrics that read more like a romance novel, such as *"And He tells me I am His own."*

"Love Song for a Savior"—*"She will come running, and fall in His arms."*

"Just to Be with You"—*"I'd give anything . . . There's no price I wouldn't pay."*

"More Like Falling in Love"—*"More like losing my heart than giving my allegiance."*

"Breathe"—*"I'm desperate for you."*

There is no mistaking this imagery, for it is indeed one of intimacy. But this teaching that reflects an intimate portrayal of one's relationship with Jesus goes far beyond the church's desire to encourage Christians to have a deeper relationship.

This is about control. Religious patriarchy is now operating in full force to control its followers.

Sitting there that day and reflecting on these teachings of Jesus and the role patriarchy played in them threatened to spiral me away from doing the work to deconstruct them. This was going to be messy and multilayered. As I began untangling the toxic web that my relationship with Jesus had been entombed in all these years, I began to understand why I couldn't bring myself to reach into the corners of my deconstruction to face this question.

What I needed to do about Jesus was far more complicated than answering, "Do you believe in God?" because the Jesus in my story was the lover that I had left without saying goodbye. The notion that I owed Jesus a goodbye may sound ridiculous. Yet even more ridiculous was discovering that I was carrying guilt about it.

If you were raised in a high-control evangelical/fundamentalist faction of Christianity, then you probably understand what I was experiencing. Without that context, it would be challenging to understand how religious patriarchy digs deep into your person's psyche until you are convinced that your soul is in great danger living apart from it. The courage to step away from it to listen to others' voices and learn from other wisdom keepers is beyond measure.

But that's the entire reason religious patriarchy is a well-oiled machine, clearly intended to keep you from stepping out in courage. Living in fear is acceptable to them if you continue to support the perpetuation of the system.

The system is the church.

What better way to continue to control the indoctrinated, especially the women, than to invoke strong feelings of romance and link that to your salvation? If your relationship with Jesus is viewed as a love story, one where you have taken vows to Him through the sacrament of baptism and confessions of faith, then it's highly unlikely that you will break those vows and reject Jesus as your intimate partner.

After all, the Bible is clear about male authority, and who is a higher authority in your life than Jesus?

As I continued to dig in that corner of my religious heritage, determined to answer this question once and for all, I came face-to-face with what I had always known but also feared.

There was nothing I could salvage from the Jesus of my religious heritage.

It was time to let Him go and heal the abyss where His presence had once been.

But Seriously, What Am I Going to Do About Jesus?

In the time since I dug into that corner of my deconstruction to discover my complicated relationship with Jesus and religious patriarchy, I've come to embrace the question, "What am I going to do about Jesus?" as part of my spiritual journey.

I've dug deep into the scholars' teachings, some that say Jesus didn't exist. Still there are others that say He did.

There is also irrefutable evidence that the Bible has been amended multiple times to include things Jesus didn't say and things He didn't do.

About now someone will want to dive into a heated debate with me to "prove it" and "cite my sources" because "Jesus is the way, the truth, and the life." My response to those critics?

No.

I won't "prove it," and I won't "cite my sources." I've never once held myself out to be a scholar of Christianity, although my education is far more extensive than the average evangelical pastor whose only qualification is having the same last name as the head pastor.

The very people who ridicule my credentials are sitting in the pews listening to a pastor whose only credentials *may* be a few years at a Bible college, yet I'm the one ill-equipped.

But I digress.

I know these critics because I was trained by them. I knew when I spiraled out of Christianity what the attack would look like and who would be making it—the Christian threatened by my story and the empowerment that story offers to others.

My shelves are filled with books from Marcus Borg, Elaine Pagels, John Shelby Spong, Rob Bell, Reza Aslan, Bart Ehrman, and many more. By comparison, the Christian who is offended by those who challenge the veracity of the Bible—especially how it pertains to the Jesus story—has most likely never read a book by any of these authors. But I've read the evangelical Christians' books. I've sat through hundreds of hours of Bible studies. I've even led some of those studies. And therein lies the biggest difference. Based on my own studies and experience from both perspectives, I can confidently say that the Jesus story is indeed inconsistent at best and highly suspect at worst.

But is that the end of the story?

Hardly. Because a Christian can read the exact same books I have read and sit through the exact same Bible studies that I have sat through and come away with an entirely different belief. It happens every day.

What does this mean for you? It means you too should be doing your own research, discovering your own wisdom keepers, and discerning what is your truth.

We can look back at Jesus with a new set of eyes to see that His ministry was never about starting a new religion. Instead, it was about stretching the constrictions that had been placed on His own religion—Judaism. He did this by pushing back on the elements of His faith that had become corrupt, dogmatic, and prejudiced against non-Jews.

The birth of Christianity came about for many reasons, and our questioning of its origins is not sacrilegious—it's freeing. What is sacrilegious are those who use their Christian identity as validation for their persecution, condemnation, and dehumanization of others.

Allegiance to a belief should not take precedence over our responsibility to humanity. As tough as that ideology may be for some, it is—I believe—the way of Jesus. It is the Jesus we see when we take His words as an invitation to embrace all our siblings, regardless of skin color, birthplace, gender identity, who they love, and even what they believe.

The deconstruction journey is less about what you believe on the other side of deconstructing—it's about who you are. Inside my inner circles are people who have deconstructed to atheism and others who remained evangelical Christians. That may seem counter to what you might expect, and you may be asking, "How can someone remain an evangelical Christian after deconstructing?"

We'll answer that in our final chapter.

But this may help.

I'm still in love with Jesus, but not the Jesus of my religious heritage and certainly not in the eerily creepy romantic way that my faith had *taught* me to be.

I'm still inspired by His teachings, but not because I need His teachings to reinforce my beliefs.

I've released Jesus to the age in which He existed, accepting that I may never know beyond a reasonable doubt what the truth is about who He was.

And This Is Where It Gets Complicated and Deeply Personal, Because for Me

I need Jesus to be real.

I was taught to focus on the miracles that surrounded Him, but when I do, His teachings about how we are to live *here,* in the *now,* fade into the background.

I need the Jesus who was

the social justice advocate;

outspoken for the oppressed;

fearless, who knew He was risking His life when He spoke out against authority;

kindhearted, who extended compassion in radical ways in a caste system that tossed people aside like garbage.

I need *this* Jesus to be real.

This is the Jesus I still seek.

To debate the parts of His story that have become weaponized is meaningless. It simply serves the religious patriarchy whose very existence is contingent upon their control of the Jesus narrative. The Jesus story extends beyond the confines of religion and is offered as a healing balm to all of humanity to remind us that things can be different when we expect them to be. For Jesus, that meant resisting the elements of His faith that had become broken, choosing instead to sit with the outcast, heal the untouchable, and act against corruption that marginalized the poor.

I still capitalize His pronouns because they reflect the part of my religious heritage with which I have reconciled.

I've rescued Jesus from religious patriarchy and returned Him to my life story because He makes my spiritual journey more meaningful.

I have no problem accepting His divinity, because He said what is in Him is also in me.

Who He was is also who I am.

That means we are all Divine.

What am I going to do about Jesus?

I'm going to embrace the parts of His story that are for the world and release the ones that oppress it.

I'm going to be open to learning new things about Him, and when what I know proves to be false, I will keep seeking to understand why revisionists changed His story throughout time.

I'll remain committed to modeling my life from the one who pushed back on systems of oppression.

This I can be sure.

He would have wanted it that way.

Reimagine the Familiar

The following list came to me as I was seeking to find the words to describe the experience of letting go of beliefs that no longer served my highest good:

Releasing

Redefining

Reconstructing

Rethinking

Reconnecting

Reconciliation

They all work, and one may resonate more with you than the other. That is a meaningful concept when you are deconstructing yet trying to find paths back to your religious heritage without the dogma, the pain, and the power structure.

When we are asking ourselves questions, like "Where is God?" or "What am I going to do about Jesus?" we must be willing to accept that our answers may change over time. Those changes signal growth. The words we use to describe this process are intricately bound to our spiritual truths and our healing journeys. It isn't uncommon that the words will change over time as well. Try some of them on. See how they fit. If they don't, move on. Trust that you will be able to find the words that best describe who you are and where you are on your spiritual journey. No one has the right to judge you for this experience, although some may try. Those who have been conditioned to believe that it is within their God-given power to do so rarely miss the opportunity to judge. Little by little and day by day, you will become more assured with your words that honor your truth and establish your boundaries.

Always remember that *not* answering someone's questions about your faith and your deconstructing is an option. That too takes courage. Do what is comfortable for you.

What follows are some insights and suggestions for *reimagining the familiar*, my chosen phrase for reexamining my beliefs and values postdeconstruction.

When I recently taught about reimagining the familiar, I offered this imagery to my students:

Imagine that you have been sewing a beautiful tapestry that is your life. This is a dance of sacred moments, intertwined together that when viewed individually do not tell the whole story of your life. Rather when the weaving begins to grow, the story takes shape. There are no mistakes in this tapestry, only lessons from which we learn. They offer us new ways to weave into our story how we changed and healed from those mistakes and lived experiences.

Same for our deconstructing of our religious heritage. As we deconstruct old beliefs and perceptions, we're not tearing apart our tapestry but rather reimagining it. This process allows us to create a spiritual journey that's not just about mending gaps but about cherishing the beauty in every twist and turn, recognizing that it's our imperfections that often make our tapestry most vibrant and authentic. And with that new insight and awareness, we keep weaving the tapestry. Now we add more vibrant colors and intricate patterns because we are no longer bound to rules that told us we weren't free to create the tapestry. When that power was within us all along.

This imagery is how I view reimagining the familiar. It is like taking a well-worn, beloved tapestry that is uniquely us and about finding new translations and understandings within the age-old narratives and traditions that have long shaped us. Many of us grew up entrenched in specific religious doctrines, but over time, as we evolve and grow, these teachings might no longer resonate with our inner truths. Yet this doesn't mean we have to discard them entirely. Instead, we can sift through these beliefs, holding on to the threads that still speak to our souls, while weaving in new insights and understandings. This journey is about honoring where we come from, recognizing the beauty in our spiritual heritage, and molding it to better align with our current truths. It's not about rejection but transformation; not about losing faith but deepening it in a way that's authentic to who we've become.

It's about releasing what the church told you your relationship with Jesus must look like.

It's about redefining who you are and embracing your spiritual identity.

It's about reconstructing after what you thought was true comes crumbling down around you.

It's about rethinking your commitment to your religious heritage, letting go of what no longer serves you, and holding on to the things that honor your spiritual authenticity.

It's about reconnecting and reclaiming your spirituality so that no part of it is ever filtered through a system that negated your control of it.

It's about reconciliation—the sweet, healing balm of coming full circle and stepping forth into your life with spiritual empowerment and peace.

Find your spiritual path, and the words that help you define it will arrive.

Trust the journey.

When we are reimagining the familiar of our religious heritage, it is important that we take our time as we peel back the layers of our indoctrinated beliefs and their impact on our lives. This is the primary process of deconstructing.

You will also want to research the ways that best serve your deconstructing process. Some people prefer to find community, while others want to just be left alone in their thoughts and feelings. There are books and courses, podcasts, and live teachings—all specifically targeting deconstruction. Feel free to explore some of my offerings at revkarla.com.

Consider a few aspects of your religious heritage that you may want to explore as you reimagine the familiar and reconcile with it in meaningful ways.

In evangelical, high-control Christian denominations, the relationship with Jesus is often described in deeply personal and intimate terms. It's framed not just as belief in a historical figure or a distant deity but as a living, dynamic relationship with the Savior of the world.

There are some common expressions and sentiments shared by individuals in these denominations. These expressions highlight the deeply personal and transformative nature of the relationship evangelicals describe with Jesus. It's a bond often characterized by gratitude, dependence, love, and a desire to align one's life with what one believes are His teachings and desires.

Below are some ways that people often describe their relationship with Jesus. These may still be meaningful to you, or you may be ready to release them. Remember, there are no wrong answers, and your answers most likely will change over time. Revisiting these periodically can be a part of your deconstructing journey, turning it into a spiritual practice that helps you see firsthand your spiritual transformation. If at any time you feel triggered by any of these, please step away and return when you feel you are ready.

Personal Salvation

"I was lost before I found Jesus."

"Jesus saved me from my sins."

Intimate Relationship

"Jesus is my best friend."

"I talk to Jesus every day."

Healing and Transformation

"Jesus healed my broken heart."

"By His stripes, I am healed."

Surrender and Devotion

"I've surrendered my life to Christ."

"I live for Jesus."

Guidance and Dependence

"I seek Jesus's will in everything I do."

"I lean on Him in times of trouble."

Evangelism and Witnessing

"I want to share the love of Jesus with others."

"He's called me to spread the Good News."

This list is not comprehensive. It's offered here as an example of the types of beliefs you may want to explore. It isn't uncommon to not have an opinion, belief, or feeling about some of these statements. Sometimes as we deconstruct, we're unraveling from our religious heritage so quickly that we are letting go of these beliefs in rapid succession.

Also remember that letting go of beliefs does not mean you are letting go of Jesus. It means you are reimagining what the Jesus story means to you when you have healed from religious patriarchy and harmful religious indoctrinations.

The indoctrinated teachings about Jesus, especially in more fundamentalist or high-control Christian denominations, can reinforce religious patriarchy in various ways.

To conclude this chapter, we'll highlight other aspects of your religious heritage that are worth considering. I recommend you take the entirety of this chapter in small bites, inviting the pause to give space for your heart and mind to help you deconstruct your first response, which may be a conditioned response from your religious heritage. Whatever works for you as you reimagine the familiar, may these help guide you with gentleness and care.

Jesus in a Hierarchical Structure

→ Jesus is often depicted as the ultimate authority figure, with all believers expected to submit to His will.

→ This hierarchy of most traditional denominations places men in roles of spiritual leadership, implying their God-ordained role in church leadership.

→ Does Jesus as an authoritarian speak to you? If no, why not? If yes, how and why?

Spiritual Experience with Jesus

→ The belief that Jesus wants a personal relationship can sometimes be used to bypass individual conscience or autonomy.

→ Does a personal relationship with Jesus resonate with your spirituality? If no, why not? If yes, how and why?

Personal Savior

→ When they are taught that Jesus is the sole source of salvation, love, or fulfillment, adherents might become emotionally dependent, making it easier for patriarchal structures to exert influence.

→ Does Jesus as your personal Savior resonate with your spirituality? If no, why not? If yes, how and why?

Interpretation of Scriptures

→ Passages emphasizing Jesus's authority, male leadership, or women's submission might be given more attention than those emphasizing love, equality, or liberation.

→ A strict, literal interpretation of certain Bible verses can support patriarchal views, especially if contextual nuances are overlooked.

→ Do the teachings that reinforce patriarchy resonate with your spirituality? If no, why not? If yes, how and why?

Heretical Labels

→ Any theological perspectives that challenge patriarchal views might be labeled as "heretical" or "outside true doctrine," even if they offer a kinder and more compassionate interpretation of Jesus.

→ Gatekeeping—there can be an active effort to keep congregants away from progressive theology or feminist interpretations of scriptures.

→ Does labeling some teachings outside of Christianity resonate with your spirituality? If no, why not? If yes, why?

Model of Suffering

→ Jesus's suffering and sacrifice can sometimes be used to encourage adherents to endure hardships or injustices, including those imposed by patriarchy.

→ Emphasizing Jesus as a martyr can promote a culture where

personal sacrifice (often expected more from women) is seen as a spiritual virtue.

→ Does Jesus's suffering and sacrifice resonate with your spirituality? If no, why not? If yes, why?

Seeing Jesus as a Spiritual Guide

→ Rather than a figure demanding obedience, we can understand Jesus as a guide, leading us toward a deeper spiritual understanding.

→ Embracing the Divine Feminine: Many mystical traditions emphasize balancing the Divine Masculine with the Divine Feminine. This balance allows a more holistic approach to spirituality, making it more inclusive and encompassing.

→ Does the teaching of the Divine Feminine resonate with your spirituality? If no, why not? If yes, how and why?

→ Are you willing to explore the Jesus story outside of the literal interpretation of the Bible, examining the virgin birth narrative, the crucifixion, the resurrection, Jesus as the Messiah, the second coming, Jesus with women leaders as disciples, and His features that are often displayed as white-centric? If no, why not? If yes, how and why?

In his book *Resurrecting Jesus: Embodying the Spirit of a Revolutionary Mystic*, the spiritual teacher Adyashanti offers ways to reimagine the familiar when it comes to your understanding of and relationship with Jesus.

Adyashanti suggests focusing on Jesus's teachings, where much of what He taught has relevance today. Then examine closely the pockets of compassion weaving through each of Jesus's teachings. Finally, consider how we can emulate those teachings in our lives by offering kindness and compassion to community through acts of service and to ourselves through meditation. This simple practice helped affirm my early path of deconstructing by allowing me to break down reimagining into manageable parts that didn't overwhelm me.

There's only one guarantee that Jesus gave: if you can receive and awaken and embody what he is speaking about, then your life will never be the same again. Then you will realize that you're already living in the Kingdom of Heaven.[1]

Reimagining the familiar can be challenging. When you have been taught to give your life to Jesus, yet you no longer recognize the aspects of yourself that were bound by those beliefs, deconstructing from this may sometimes feel as if you are losing a significant part of your identity. The truth is you are.

Let me offer this one final thought.

What if instead of asking, "What am I going to do about Jesus?" we ask ourselves, "Why have I never seen how inspired I can be by the Jesus story without being bound to toxic theology?"

That's where we find the real Jesus.

I'll close with the words of Bishop John Shelby Spong, whose writings got me through some of the most challenging times of my own deconstructing. May they inspire you and remind you that you are not alone. You are standing on the shoulders of giants who paved the way for us to hopefully make the work of deconstructing easier, helping us to land gently into the ground with a newfound spiritual identity that serves our highest good.

I pray that for you, Beloved.

> Yet even understanding these things, I am still attracted to this Jesus, and I will pursue him both relentlessly and passionately. I will not surrender the truth I believe I find in him either to those who seek to defend the indefensible or to those who want to be freed finally from premodern ideas that no longer make any sense.
>
> —John Shelby Spong

Beloved,

Demolish. Repair. Restore.
Once we have demolished our old faith structure and repaired the harm the church has done, it isn't uncommon

to sense a longing to begin the rebuilding of our spirituality.

When that occurs, we have reached the restorative phase.

Reimagining Jesus is restorative.

I want to caution you that people reach this phase at different points—some never reach it. Revisiting old beliefs and dredging through triggering memories is just too painful.

If the timing doesn't feel right, do not press into these journaling. Forcing our way through deconstructing puts us at risk of missing key elements of our healing.

Remember, deconstructing isn't static. It isn't linear. There is no timeline. You may feel the need to skip this altogether and still reclaim your spirituality in a way that serves your well-being.

Then again—one day, you may find yourself wondering, "What am I going to do about Jesus?"

If and when that comes, may this chapter and these suggested exercises be exactly what you need.

REFLECTIVE QUESTIONS AND JOURNALING PROMPTS

→ *How does your personal history and experience with Jesus align with what you now believe about Jesus?*

→ *In what ways can you view Jesus as a moral or spiritual guide rather than a Savior figure, and how does that alter your relationship with His teachings and His impact on your life?*

→ *What aspects of Jesus's message resonate with you?*

→ *How can the concept of Jesus as a revolutionary, who challenged social norms and advocated for the marginalized, influence your actions and beliefs today?*

TIMELINE EXERCISE

→ *Create a timeline of Jesus's life based on the Gospels. Attempting to put everything on this timeline would be overwhelming. Choose aspects of Jesus's life that resonate with you—stories you remember as a child to specific things He said or parables He told.*

→ *Next to each event or teaching, write down how that resonates with your own values and experiences.*

→ *Reflect on this timeline and note any emotions or thoughts that arise.*

→ *Consider how this humanistic approach to Jesus's life might inform your current spiritual practices or ethical outlook.*

→ *As you move through your deconstructing journey, revisit this timeline occasionally to see if your relationship changes with what you included and how your perspectives on aspects of Jesus's life have changed.*

9

Life After Deconstructing

Living a Spiritually Empowered Life

What About You?

We're going to take a turn here and get a little mystical. Come along with me as we explore this question and what it means to reclaim your spirituality.

In this book's introduction, I asked this question: "What about you?" I invited you to consider if this spiritual struggle that you were experiencing was an inner knowing to enter into deconstructing your religious heritage.

Now, I invite you to consider "What about you?" as in "Who do you say *you* are?"

I called myself an unchurched, nonconforming Christian who walks the spiritual-but-not-religious path. When I add that I'm also an ordained interfaith/interspiritual minister, it's easy to see why people can be confused about who I am and what I believe.

I've learned to be okay with that. I've had my fill of catchy and trendy phrases that were used as marketing gimmicks inside evangelical Christianity. Who wasn't caught up in the trend to stop calling ourselves a Christian, opting instead for "Christ Follower," a phrase that was supposed to signify our steadfastness to the "true" message of Christ. Or "WWJD," another campaign that became heavily influenced by evangelical Christianity to signify

the followers who were willing to be seen as the "true" followers. And of course, there were "radical" Christians, inspired by
the book of the same name by David Platt. Platt, an evangelical
pastor, urged believers to return to a more authentic and biblical understanding of Jesus's teachings, one that necessitates radical self-denial, sacrificial giving, and a profound commitment to
global missions.

All these gimmicks were simply evangelical Christianity's response to a world that was quickly changing and leaving its values
and beliefs behind.

But that's just me. Perhaps those are triggers that I'll work
through, and I'll one day settle into a one- or two-word description of who I am. Many people do just that.

Spiritual seeker.

Spiritually independent.

Spiritual nomad or wanderer.

A "none" (spiritual but not religious).

An SBNR (spiritual but not religious).

And so on.

That is the beauty of a liberated spirituality that is no longer
beholden to a system that requires its leadership's approval. Finding your identity can be as simple as trying on a few descriptors to
see what fits. It can also change as you continue your deconstruction journey. In fact, I would expect it to do just that.

"Nonconforming Christian" is an important part of my identity
because I desire to hold onto elements of my religious heritage as
a nod to my spiritual journey. Many people do that as well. They
become Christian Buddhists, Christian mystics, Christian witches,
and so on. When one has been freed from the identities regulated
by organized religion, infinite possibilities arrive to be considered,
tried on, integrated, and celebrated.

I'm smiling as I type this because this is indeed liberating.

Depending on how meaningful this is to you, spend time looking at these titles and research others to see what resonates with

you. I discovered the concept of nonconforming in a 1955 sermon by Rev. Dr. Martin Luther King Jr.

Dr. King references the verse from Romans 12:2, where Paul wrote: "Do not conform to the pattern of this world but be transformed by the renewing of your mind. Then you will be able to test and approve what God's will is—his good, pleasing and perfect will."

If you grew up evangelical, this verse was pounded into your head as a call to resist the secular culture, which was in opposition to the teachings of the Bible. In this context, church authority was also emphasized, meaning that there was no greater authority in the Christian's life than God first, then church authority second. This clearly gave church leaders carte blanche to interpret scripture in a slant that favored this position.

Yet Dr. King, a Baptist minister himself, came to a very different conclusion of what transforming and nonconforming meant to the Christian. He wrote:

> Only through an inner spiritual transformation do we gain the strength to fight vigorously the evils of the world in a humble and loving spirit. The transformed nonconformist, moreover, never yields to the passive sort of patience that is an excuse to do nothing. And this very transformation saves him from speaking irresponsible words that estrange without reconciling and from making hasty judgments that are blind to the necessity of social progress. He recognizes that social change will not come overnight, yet he works as though it is an imminent possibility.
>
> This hour in history needs a dedicated circle of transformed nonconformists.[1]

I cried reading his words. In his teaching, I had discovered a connection to the Christians who used their faith to fight for equity and justice, and I felt a kindredship and validation for the work that I do as part of my ministry.

And so, I became a nonconforming Christian to honor Dr. King and to remain connected to my Christian heritage.

While the process of finding a descriptor for your spiritual identity may be healing and liberating for you, it is not necessary. Do not force this. Nothing on this deconstructing journey should be forced.

This is a new era, and it requires a new way of thinking—a new way of approaching the work of spirituality.

This is how we heal, reclaim our spirituality, and live spiritually empowered lives.

What Is a Spiritually Empowered Life?

Somewhere in our evangelical Christian experience, we gave up some level of control of our spirituality. We did this willingly. It was framed as a necessary part of our path to salvation. "Giving our lives to Christ" meant surrendering our right to spiritual autonomy. You may have never thought of it this way, but consider the answers you might give to the following questions:

Did you hesitate asking questions that revealed doubts you may have been having about your faith for fear of being rebuked by church leaders?

Did you witness favoritism by church leaders but kept silent for fear that church leaders would be angry with you?

Do you recall hearing sermons where pastors demonized world religions by calling their beliefs heretical or mocked their spiritual practices?

Were you told that if you did not get baptized you would go to hell?

Were you taught that a tithe meant a tenth of your gross income and giving less could bring the wrath of God upon you?

Were you instructed to support the world missionaries that the church sponsored as a part of your responsibility as a Christian?

Were you scolded, either in person or in sermons, for not inviting more people to church as part of your evangelical responsibilities?

Answering yes to any of these questions could indicate that surrendering some element of our spiritual autonomy was a requirement of our inclusion in our church communities. Oftentimes, these high-control churches tell us what to believe, how to worship, and how we show up in our lives. When we begin to deconstruct, we may not initially be aware that what we are in essence doing is reclaiming our spirituality, but indeed that is what we are doing.

Based on my experiences and those of countless others who have shared their stories with me, I've compiled a list that encapsulates wisdom we gathered and experiences we had as we worked to reclaim our spirituality. Keep in mind that this list is not arbitrary, and it is not comprehensive. Everyone's experience is unique. However, there are enough elements of commonality in our journeys that I feel this list will be helpful as your deconstruction journey brings you through the demolishing of the harmful elements of your religious heritage and into restoring your spirituality in a sacred way.

Spirituality Is More Individual than We Were Taught

Let's be very clear here. Individual spirituality isn't the same as individualism—a viewpoint of right-leaning conservative Christians and Christian nationalists that asserts that individual rights, freedoms, and responsibilities should take precedence over the needs or dictates of the state or social groups. Advocates of this philosophy often argue for limited government intervention in personal lives and economic affairs, believing that individual freedom and autonomy are crucial for prosperity and societal well-being. This stance is highly controversial and quite hypocritical in that the stance of limited government intervention only applies to how that government intervention impacts the rights of conservative Christians. People who support this ideology have no issue whatsoever forcing their beliefs through advocating for Bible teachings in schools, book banning, and the loss of women's rights to agency over their bodies.

Individual spirituality is the belief that each person possesses a spirituality that is as personal and unique as our individual DNA. This spirituality is influenced by our ancestral heritage, our lived experiences, and our inner knowing of what our true and authentic paths are. When we deconstruct from high-control religious experience, this concept often feels isolating and intimidating. Yet if we trust the deconstruction process, we soon learn that reclaiming our spirituality doesn't exclude us from existing in a community setting where we are surrounded by people who respect our individual spiritual identities. Once we embrace this concept, we feel a sense of liberation that plants us firmly on a path to healing.

Spirituality Is Not Religion; Religion Is Not Spirituality

This may seem like a no-brainer for many of us who have walked this path for a while. Or perhaps you have never considered how you use the words *spirituality* and *religion*. Oftentimes, they are used interchangeably, and depending on your religious heritage, their interchangeable use is intentional. If we view spirituality and religion as one and the same, then the definitions of both become murky. For high-control religious organizations like evangelical Christianity, this is beneficial, for if you believe that they are the same, then it is easy to assume that one cannot exist without the other.

Reclaiming your spirituality means you now understand that the difference between the two is succinctly different. Even if you remain in the church or decide to return after your season of deconstructing, understanding these definitions ensures that you cannot be spiritually manipulated to believe otherwise.

Spirituality pertains to an individual's personal experience and connection with the Divine, higher power, or greater purpose, or your experience with who or what God is. It often focuses on inner growth, understanding, and the essence of being and can be experienced both within and outside formal religious contexts.

Religion is an organized system of beliefs, practices, rituals, and symbols centered around a higher power or deity (or deities). It usually encompasses specific doctrines, sacred texts, and communal worship, often providing a structured community and moral framework for its adherents. Religion is a conduit by which your spirituality may be nurtured, but it is not a requirement for your spirituality.

Expressions of Faith Through Rituals, Worship, and Spiritual Practices Are Personal

"You're supposed to . . ."

How many times have you been instructed on how to pray, how to worship, how to dress, and so on? Reclaiming your spirituality means you are invited to embrace practices and rituals that genuinely resonate with your spirituality, rather than having those practices imposed on you by traditions or customs. That isn't to say that traditions or customs aren't available to you to integrate into your rituals. They absolutely are. Holistic integration, however, means you integrate those rituals into your daily life as well as special events or occasions throughout the year. It's a more expansive and fluid approach to expressing your faith, and it often allows others who are less familiar with your beliefs to participate in a nonintimidating way.

Community Isn't Contingent Upon Shared Beliefs

Finding or creating a supportive, open-minded community where diverse spiritual journeys are respected and celebrated is a benefit that many of us have discovered on our deconstructing journeys. The community takes on a more expansive meaning, with opportunities to connect with people through virtual connection but also reimagining what gatherings look like locally. These communities will continue to blossom as more and more people reclaim their spirituality and reimagine what sacred gatherings will be outside of organized religion.

Embracing Uncertainty

I mentioned this above, but it's worth repeating here—questioning what is real and what is true about faith and spirituality can in and of itself be a complete spiritual journey. Recognizing that the spiritual journey isn't always clear-cut, and being open to ambiguity, questions, and evolving understandings invites an openness to be curious and a commitment to live with wonder.

Living Without Spiritual Silos

"I want to live silo-less. I don't want to live in a silo. I don't want my spirituality to be tied to just one silo."

I hadn't planned to say this during a recent workshop on reclaiming your spirituality, but it resonated so deeply with the attendees that I shared it here. Evangelical Christianity demanded that its silo of beliefs, values, and rules be the one that governs our lives. When we deconstruct and reclaim our spirituality, many of us climb out of that silo and made a commitment to live silo-less, opting instead to learn about and experience some of the spiritual traditions from around the world. Living silo-less isn't a free pass to appropriate others' traditions without permission, especially if they are closed practices (spiritual practices that are only available to those who are a part of that tradition—often seen in Indigenous cultures).

There is a vast array of spiritual traditions and beliefs, and learning from them can be enriching and rewarding. Spirituality in a silo restricts our understanding of and respect for other beliefs and traditions.

Reclaiming your spirituality may offer you a heart-expanding, soul-integrating experience. This is the spirit dancing. It's complete and utter freedom without rules and regulations on how you are now free to embrace this spirituality that is yours. There is something inherently sacred about proclaiming, "It is time for me to just dive deep into this sacred work and reclaim my spirituality and live with spiritual authenticity."

It is when we make this commitment that we begin to live a spiritually empowered life.

Who Was I Before the World Told Me Otherwise?

Living a spiritually empowered life is not a new concept. It has been around for years. Of course, religion has found ways to bind it to their teachings, and some factions of new age spirituality often minimize it to mean "just do what feels good." But living a spiritually empowered life extends far beyond the constraints of organized religion or the simplified ideology of some new age teachings.

Living a spiritually empowered life means staying connected to your inner knowing, your source of strength, for guidance and purpose. Simply put, it means your inner wisdom is just as wise and powerful as anything on the outside of you. When you are doing the work to reclaim your spirituality and heal from lived experiences, your inner wisdom deserves the same level of respect that you may give to wisdom teachers, counselors, and sages.

For someone deconstructing Christianity and moving away from a patriarchal understanding of God, living a spiritually empowered life is more than just a journey of self-discovery. It's about seeking a more authentic, inclusive, and personal connection with the Divine or your understanding of who or what God is.

In short, living a spiritually empowered life can be said to be the outward expression of reclaiming your spirituality. Outward is more than just the physical aspect of displaying spiritual empowerment. A person does not have to make bold proclamations of faith or belief. It doesn't even mean that people may witness a person living spiritually empowered. It means that an individual is making choices on their life's direction, priorities, boundaries, and values based on the work that brought them to that point.

Living a spiritually empowered life means using discernment and never acquiescing to a perceived power structure based on systems that a person has deconstructed. It's a continual commitment to do the work to remain diligent to protect one's values but also to remain open-minded and open-hearted to release what arrives that no longer serves the true self—the soul.

Remember—I did say this chapter would be mystical.

Take a breath and continue this journey with me for just a moment longer, because we are closing out our time together. This book would be much longer if I attempted to expand on each of these concepts.

For you, Beautiful Soul, what is important is that you are not afraid of the deconstructing journey and also find hope when you have done that hard work of deconstruction.

These concepts are here because you will now hear about them everywhere. It's funny how that works, isn't it? When the student is ready, the teacher will arrive. You'll hear about reclaiming your spirituality, living with spiritual empowerment, and what the true self is, and perhaps you'll feel less intimidated and perhaps a tad hopeful that you're going to be okay.

And you are going to be okay.

This I can assure you.

Let us close our time in this chapter with this final teaching on the true self. The true self is the part of us who knows who we are simply because we are here. This true self assures us that our worth isn't contingent upon our physical attributes, our wealth, our intelligence, or our status.

None of those matter. Those are outward-facing aspects of us that are the results of our work or simply our lot in life. The true self inherently knows that all manner of things are good and deserving of love and respect, including us.

When we begin to recognize our worth by becoming aware of our true selves, living spiritually empowered becomes almost second nature. Things that used to matter will fall away. We start to notice that triggers we've had our entire lives simply evoke no response from us. Free from forced silence through religious patriarchy, we discover that silence can be empowering when we have stated our boundaries and feel no need to defend them against those attempting to manipulate us.

We feel physically lighter because we aren't carrying the weight of guilt and shame that was never ours to carry.

We see God in the world and the Holy in the everyday.

And we reimagine the familiar in our lives—those things that suffocated us, controlled us, silenced us, harmed us, yet we are bound to them in ways that beckon us to build bridges over the troubled waters of our lived experiences. "What would this look like?" you ask.

Where we had no desire for a ritual that reminds us of our religious heritage, we reimagine the familiar by lighting a candle and marveling at the sacred in the simplicity of the dancing light.

We invite a group of women who are deconstructing to lead a midnight service on Christmas Eve, and we reimagine the familiar for a service that only men could officiate in your faith tradition.

We decline an in-person invitation to a family gathering where our beliefs and values are mocked, and we reimagine the familiar by visiting a long-lost friend who has been our cheerleader during our deconstructing.

We write a rage letter* to the person who caused us great harm in our past, then we reimagine the familiar by writing a rage letter to our pastor, who taught us that forgiveness without restoration of a relationship meant we were sinning because we now understand that this teaching served the patriarchy by gaslighting victims of abuse into believing that garbage.

Reimagining the familiar is a sacred tool for living a spiritually empowered life. It's about finding fresh perspectives within the age-old narratives and traditions that have long shaped us.

It's about finally being able to answer that question: "Who was I before the world told me otherwise?"

Truthfully, with conviction and passion.

This is what it means to live a spiritually empowered life that reflects your true self.

Finally—Trust the Journey

Beloved, I wish I could wave a magic wand and show you what lies ahead and what the result will be. If you trust this journey, perhaps you too will discover that this can change you in ways that you had not expected and spiritually empower you in ways you never could have imagined.

I can say this—I have never met anyone who has regretted deconstructing. Yes, it is true that it may lead us away from our religious heritage, but in its place, we have found a true peace that's almost too hard to describe. That alone makes this all worth it.

I pray this for you, as well.

What I have discovered is that without a deep commitment to unlearning and detangling from the elements of Christianity that harmed you, those indoctrinated beliefs and biases are the filter through which you will continue to view life and the world around you.

In other words, without actively deconstructing, you will still be led by your trauma, your biases, and your prejudices that are deeply ingrained in your indoctrinated beliefs. It won't matter if you choose atheism or want to explore how the Divine ebbs and flows throughout creation. I've personally experienced this and have witnessed it with others. This is the important difference—rejecting your faith and walking away from church may relieve the pain, but only deconstruction will ensure those experiences have no power over you.

It is about healing, but it is also about unlearning, detangling, and deprogramming.

Make a commitment to do the work.

I'm cheering for you from here.

Beloved,

Demolish. Repair. Restore.

REFLECTIVE QUESTIONS AND JOURNALING PROMPTS

→ *What spiritual practices or beliefs have consistently resonated with you, even as you've moved away from traditional Christianity?*

→ *Can you identify moments or experiences where you felt a deep connection to something greater than yourself? How did these experiences shape your understanding of spirituality?*

→ *Reflect on the labels you've used to define your faith in the past. How do they align or contrast with your current spiritual understanding?*

→ *How do you envision the expression of your spirituality in daily life? What values, practices, or communities align with this vision?*

TIMELINE EXERCISE

Consider writing a spiritual autobiography to your timeline. This exercise involves chronicling your spiritual journey from as early as you can remember to the present day. Highlight key moments of transformation, doubt, revelation, and growth. This process can help you see patterns, identify core beliefs, and articulate how you've evolved.

Epilogue

Toward the end of writing this book, something happened that triggered so many emotions about my deconstructing journey. I'm sharing it here because I think it will help you understand the importance of committing to deconstructing to reclaim your spirituality.

When I was a passionate evangelical Christian, contemporary Christian music was, as they say, my jam. It was the only music I listened to and the only concerts I attended. Third Day, Newsboys, Hillsong United, MercyMe, Jesus Culture. I knew every song. If they were in concert within a few hours' drive from our home, we were there. My playlist for everything from exercising to writing was a compilation of these songs. Our church's worship playlist was comprised of music from these artists.

To say I was completely immersed in contemporary Christian music is putting it mildly.

There was another playlist that was just as meaningful but known only to me. This playlist was comprised of songs that I had never heard played in worship. I had only seen one of the artists on that playlist in concert—Nichole Nordeman. They tended to play in smaller venues and not tour much, and Indiana didn't seem to be on their radar for concert dates.

This playlist held the songs that brought me to tears. The songs were so sacred to me that there were times when I would sit in my car and allow a song from that playlist to finish because it felt sacrilegious to cut the song midstream.

Y'all—when I say I was a Jesus freak, I mean it.

Nichole Nordeman's song "River God" invited us to visualize a stone being made smooth by the rushing waters and how that was symbolic for our lives. Oh, to be just a little smoother in the hands of the Divine at the end of my life! Will the work that I am doing leave the world a little better—or will it even matter?

Those were the thoughts that these songs evoked in me. With no one around that I could share these thoughts with, they remained unspoken but grew louder in my head as time went on.

Another artist on this private playlist was Michael Gungor. His song "Beautiful Things" would stop me in my tracks each time I heard it. The song invited us to look at how a life is made beautiful not by our outward appearance but by our desire to move closer to the Divine.

Why couldn't faith be this simple? Why couldn't we all believe that beautiful things can emerge from creation, and instead of prioritizing the ways we were different, why couldn't we connect on our common humanity?

Looking back, I can see how I was seeking out music that was rising above praise and worship music to connect with the mystical level of spirituality. This wasn't mainstream Christianity—at least not from my experience. But it felt realer, more loving.

It felt more like Jesus than anything I was finding rocking out to worship songs at a concert or at church.

These songs were pointing me to a truth that I wasn't ready to face about my spirituality—that the God of my religion, the one I was worshiping in church, was too small. Those songs were inviting me to look beyond my religious heritage, and not long after, that was exactly what I would be doing.

Fast-forward several years to just a few months ago. I was scrolling through my social media followers, which I sometimes

do as a practice of gratitude. As I was scrolling through on Instagram, I recognized the name of someone who was following me.

Michael Gungor.

Wait. What?

Was that *the* Michael Gungor?

A quick look at his profile and content revealed that it was *the*
Michael Gungor. I froze, my breath caught in my throat. Don't get
me wrong. I have several celebrity followers, and I've celebrated
each one in my own way . . . but this one.

This one was different. This one was a bridge to my religious
heritage, the one from which I fully deconstructed, yet here I
was having this visceral response to seeing his name as a follower. It had been years since I'd played his song. I felt there was
no need for it now. There was a time when it served my spirituality, but now I found meaning and comfort in other styles of music
for my meditations and practices.

Seeing his name brought back the melody of his music. And
the words. Oh, the words.

"You make beautiful things out of us."

Instantly, the tears flowed, surprising me with the flood of
emotions that accompanied them. This was reminiscent of the responses I had when I was literally losing my religion and grieving
the loss of my community, my identity, and my faith.

Why now? Why after all these years was I responding to this
moment with such raw emotion?

Why? Because, Beloved, it is just like I said earlier in this
book—deconstructing is not linear. It ebbs and flows as we discover spaces deep within ourselves where hurt still lives. Seemingly out of nowhere, the invitation arrives to allow light into
those spaces. We don't know when or how that invitation will
arrive—a phone call, a card, a video, or a new follower on your
social media platform.

Healing arrived for me in this moment, blindsiding me as I
trusted its arrival and leaned into its wisdom. I reached out to

Michael, thanking him for the follow and asking his permission to share what his music meant to me. He didn't hesitate to say of course I could share my story about his music.

It took me several more months before I was ready to share it, but this past week, I knew it was time. Michael had shared a video, expressing his desire to find a church. And although I have no right to be proud of him—he and I aren't friends off social media—I am very proud of him for making that video. In it, he not only shares his own deconstructing journey, but he also clearly lays out what his expectations are for a church that would serve his spirituality.

Feel that shift? It's easy to miss if you're not paying attention, but this is an important insight for your deconstructing journey. What Michael is doing is setting boundaries around his spiritual experience. This is what it means to reclaim your spirituality. For those of us who were taught that to be the good Christian we must contort ourselves to exist within that framework, reclaiming your spirituality means we are flipping the script. Instead of becoming what church says we must be, we show up asking how church can enrich our spiritual experience.

This, I believe, is the way it was always supposed to be. Religion, in its purest form, is a nurturer of an individual's soul. Sadly, that is not the case in many religions, including Christianity. Michael is setting an example of what it means to deconstruct by demolishing the framework that suffocated a person's spirituality, repairing the place where hurt and trauma lie, and restoring a vibrant and healed spirituality that supports one's journey and enriches one's life.

I love this for him. Some might think that I, as someone who is content as an unchurched, nonconforming Christian who walks the spiritual-but-not-religious path, might be disappointed in Michael's decision to shop for a church. Nothing could be further from the truth.

In fact, I celebrate his decision. Deconstructing is not about where you land. This is what makes the process of deconstructing so beautiful. Deconstructing is about healing, reclaiming your spirituality, then you are setting the boundaries for what your spirituality is going to look like.

Michael Gungor's music offered me a lifeline when I didn't even know I needed it. Looking back over that time, I can now see that I was pulled to the mystical language offered by artists like Michael and Nichole Nordeman, who also deconstructed elements of her evangelical faith that support Christian nationalism. Perhaps those words were calling to us all, beckoning us to come out of the silo that our faith had placed us in.

Perhaps.

Why did I choose to end with this story?

It provides a poignant placeholder for this phase of my deconstructing journey, a journey that, if I am breathing, I will continue to travel.

It was only after sharing this story that I was able to fully listen to Michael's song "Beautiful Things." As I sat there listening with my eyes closed, I had a moment of grieving what I had lost, followed by waves of immense gratitude for what I had gained after leaving the church.

Michael finding me on Instagram led to my reclaiming something that I hadn't even realized I was missing—a path back to music that still held meaning to who I am today. For Michael, his deconstructing path may lead him back to church. Michael's music affirms my decision to remain unchurched.

As I listen to the words, I'm reminded that I am indeed a beautiful thing, made beautiful not by my faith in a belief system but made beautiful because I am human.

I may no longer believe in the God of my religious heritage, but I do believe in a Divine presence that by some force of nature or Holy miracle brought me forth at this time to do as much good as I can and enjoy my life to the fullest.

I pray this for you as well, Beloved.

May your deconstructing journey bring you to a place where you believe that you not only belong but that you are a beautiful thing.

In the end, this is all that matters.

Blessed be.

SUGGESTED READING

Goddesses in Everywoman: Powerful Archetypes in Women's Lives by Jean Shinoda Bolen

Meeting Jesus Again for the First Time: The Historical Jesus and the Heart of Contemporary Faith by Marcus J. Borg

The Chalice and the Blade: Our History, Our Future by Riane Eisler

Women Who Run with the Wolves: Myths and Stories of the Wild Woman Archetype by Clarissa Pinkola Estés

The Will to Change: Men, Masculinity, and Love by bell hooks

Rev Karla's Spiritual Resources Guides by Karla Kamstra. https://revkarla.com/rev-karlas-spiritual-resource-guides/

Falling Upward: A Spirituality for the Two Halves of Life by Richard Rohr

The Universal Christ: How a Forgotten Reality Can Change Everything We See, Hope For, and Believe by Richard Rohr

Jesus for the Non-Religious: Recovering the Divine at the Heart of the Human by John Shelby Spong

Why Christianity Must Change or Die: A Bishop Speaks to Believers in Exile by John Shelby Spong

Leaving Church: A Memoir of Faith by Barbara Brown Taylor

Leaving the Fold: A Guide for Former Fundamentalists and Others Leaving Their Religion by Marlene Winell

GLOSSARY

The terms in this glossary are offered to provide context as they relate to deconstructing. While I may rely on widely accepted definitions (such as found at merriam-webster.com) for some terms, others are specific to someone seeking to understand these concepts from a deconstructing standpoint. As an example, the term *deconstructing* would be defined differently by an evangelical pastor whose objective is to disparage the deconstructing process.

Agnosticism: Agnosticism is the view that the existence of God, the Divine, or the supernatural is unknown or unknowable.

Allegory: An allegory is a story or writing that reveals a meaning, typically a moral, ethical, or political one.

Ally: An ally is a person or group that provides support and stands in solidarity with a community other than their own, particularly in the pursuit of social justice and equality. Now often used specifically for a person who is not a member of a marginalized or mistreated group but who expresses or gives support to that group.

Apostate: A label church leaders will assign to people who are no longer loyal to the beliefs of a religion, in this context Christianity. A person who rejects the teachings or the authority of Christianity are said to have committed apostasy.

Ascetism: A lifestyle of abstinence from various worldly pleasures, often with the aim of pursuing spiritual goals. People who choose a life as a monk will often take a vow to live an ascetic life.

Atheism: A disbelief in the existence of God or gods, or in a creator being.

Authoritarianism: Favoring a concentration of power in a leader or an elite not constitutionally responsible to the people. (Merriam-Webster)

Carrying Water: Carrying water refers to actions or behaviors that support and perpetuate a system of power that benefits both those in power and the one carrying the water. In the context of this book, it is referring to those who benefit by carrying water for the patriarchal system, which upholds male dominance and the oppression of others.

Christian Apologist: Someone who defends and explains a literal interpretation of Christian beliefs to uphold traditional Christian doctrine. This often means they adhere to a rigid dogma that supports a religious patriarchal structure.

Cisgender: A person whose gender identity corresponds with the sex the person was identified as having at birth. (Merriam-Webster)

Class Structure: Class structure is the organization of society into a hierarchy based on socioeconomic status, including wealth, income, education, religion, and occupation. It shapes individuals' access to resources and opportunities, creating divisions that affect lifestyle, behavior, education, and the intergenerational transmission of privileges or disadvantages.

Colonialism: Domination of a people or area by a foreign state or nation: the practice of extending and maintaining a nation's political and economic control over another people or area. (Merriam-Webster)

Complementarian Theology: Complementarian theology is a religious doctrine that is based on the belief that there are only two genders (male and female). The doctrine states that men and women have different but complementary roles and responsibilities in marriage, family life, religious leadership, and elsewhere. It posits that while both genders are equal in value and worth before God, they are destined for distinct roles, with male headship in the home and church as a key tenet. This theology is the foundation for prohibiting women to be in positions of leadership within the church.

Dark Night of the Soul: A phrase that describes a period of deep spiritual crisis, of doubt and feelings of emptiness where the individual often feels a disconnect from the Divine.

Deconstructing: The process of questioning your faith and discovering new aspects about spirituality.

Divine Feminine: The Divine Feminine represents the feminine aspects of the Divine, emphasizing qualities such as intuition, nurturing, and creation. It is often associated with attributes associated with motherhood, fertility, and the natural world. The Divine Feminine is not about gender. It is about embracing the qualities of the Divine Feminine that exists in each human.

Dualistic Framework: A dualistic framework is a structure which divides the world into two opposing parts, such as good and evil, physical and spiritual, or light and darkness. This often leads to seeing situations or people as good or bad without any room for empathy or context.

Evangelical: A branch of Christianity that is known for its focus on evangelizing their faith to encourage other people to convert to their beliefs.

Existential: Grounded in existence or the experience of existence. (Merriam-Webster)

Gatekeeping: In a spiritual context, gatekeeping refers to the act of deciding who is deemed worthy or legitimate to participate in certain religious or spiritual practices, beliefs, or communities. It often involves setting rigid boundaries around spirituality that exclude those who are not part of the spiritual community or church's membership.

Individualism: A social and political philosophy that emphasizes the moral worth, and the rights of the individual over those of the

group or collective, and places a greater emphasis on personal autonomy and self-reliance. This ideology has been co-opted by some
Christian nationalists who use it to justify suppressing opposing
views and resisting government intervention, framing their quest for
control under the guise of religious freedom. *Spiritual Individualism*
is a separation from organized religion, particularly high-control or
theologically weaponized beliefs, to facilitate healing. Unlike the
broader ideology of individualism, spiritual individualism focuses
on personal autonomy in spiritual practices and beliefs, and should
not be dismissed as merely New Age, but recognized as a valid path
to personal healing and empowerment.

Indoctrination: The process by which individuals are conditioned
to accept a set of beliefs. This type of conditioning also demands
that the beliefs not be questioned.

Inner Child Wounds: Deep-seated emotional wounds experienced
during childhood that continue to impact a person's behavior and
emotional well-being in adulthood.

Internalized Patriarchy: Internalized patriarchy refers to the uncon-
scious absorption of patriarchal values and beliefs by individuals
whose personhood is oppressed or marginalized by that patriarchal
structure. As an example, a woman may feel that women aren't
smart enough to lead because she believes in the patriarchal teaching that men are naturally better equipped to be leaders. It manifests in self-perceptions and behaviors that uphold the superiority
of masculine traits over feminine ones, often to one's own detriment
or the detriment of others. This internalization does not just impact
women. It impacts any member of a marginalized or historically
oppressed group who believes and upholds the patriarchal structure.

Mansplaining: A situation where a man explains something to
someone, typically a woman, in a manner that is condescending or
patronizing, often assuming the woman has no knowledge about
the topic. It reflects a broader issue of societal norms, where men's
voices or perspectives are privileged, and men are accustomed to
having authority over others. Men who engage in mansplaining do

not acknowledge the competency and experience of others, including when a woman may be more knowledgeable or experienced.

Martin Luther: Martin Luther was a German monk and theologian in the sixteenth century who played a pivotal role in initiating the Protestant Reformation. He challenged the authority and doctrines of the Roman Catholic Church by publishing the 95 Theses in 1517, advocating for a return to the scriptures as the sole source of religious authority and criticizing Catholic Church practices that he felt were unethical and immoral.

Megachurch: A megachurch is a Christian church that has a large number of people attending its worship services, typically numbering in the thousands. These churches will have massive resources from donations and tithes that allow them to purchase the best of products like modern technology and production equipment. Some megachurches become so large that they expand to various campuses throughout a region or establish a nationwide network. While they may offer many programs and services to their church members, megachurches have also been criticized for negatively impacting smaller churches that cannot compete with their marketing and advertising yet are often seen as more connected and integral to the local needs of the community.

Microaggression: A comment or action that subtly and often unconsciously or unintentionally expresses a prejudiced attitude toward a member of a marginalized group (such as a racial minority). (Merriam-Webster)

Monarchical System: A monarchical system is a structure in which a single person, known as a monarch, rules as the head of state, typically for life. How much power the ruling monarch has depends on the structure of the government. Some rule with absolute power, while others within the limits of a constitution. The crown typically passed down through family lines.

Mysticism: Union with the Divine through direct, personal experiences. Often characterized by experiences that are unrelated to religious beliefs or affiliations.

Nationalism: Political ideology that advocates for specific beliefs and values to influence all laws and education.

Nonconforming Christian: Someone who practices their faith in ways that diverge from traditional or mainstream Christian doctrines and church teachings. They will typically prioritize personal interpretation and experience of spirituality over institutionalized dogma. They often are not affiliated with any denomination and do not attend church with any regularity, choosing spiritual practices that support and enrich their personal spiritual journey and beliefs. Some hold onto the "Christian" identifier as a link to their religious heritage without being beholden to it.

PTSD/CPTSD: Post-traumatic stress disorder and complex post-traumatic stress disorder. Mental health conditions triggered by experiencing or witnessing tragic or terrifying events. *Complex* signifies repeated and prolonged exposure to the abuse.

Privilege/White Privilege: A special right or advantage that is available only to a particular person or group of people.

Rage Letter: A spiritual practice that can offer an emotional release, a rage letter allows individuals to express intense feelings and thoughts about a situation without restraint or fear of judgment. The practice is deeply personal and confidential, which creates a safe space to confront and purge pent-up anger, facilitating healing and offering a pathway toward inner peace.

Religious Patriarchy: A belief system and social structure within religious traditions that privileges men with authority and leadership roles while subordinating women and other historically marginalized groups of people, often using sacred texts and doctrines to justify male superiority and the suppression of rights of others which leads to inequality.

Religious Trauma: A harmful experience within a religious context.

Revictimization: A phenomenon where an individual experiences victimization, such as abuse or trauma, repeatedly in different instances or contexts.

Spirit of Offense: A phrase used to label and discredit individuals who challenge church leadership. An example is advocating for one's self or others who have been wrongly judged or accused; a church leader may say that person has a spirit of offense because they are not accepting church authority. Church leaders will often suggest that their reactions are not legitimate concerns but rather manifestations of a rebellious or overly sensitive attitude. It has been used as a mechanism to silence dissent and maintain conformity within church.

Spiritual Abuse: The exploitation of a person's faith or beliefs, often by a religious leader, to inflict harm on the individual.

Spiritual Gaslighting: A form of spiritual abuse where an individual's perception of reality is questioned by religious leaders to cause the victim to believe that they lack faith.

Spiritual Wilderness: A term that indicates the feeling of lack of foundations and direction when an individual is exploring new or different spirituality.

Toxic Theology: A harmful belief system within a religion that promotes destructive practices and causes spiritual harm.

Trauma-Informed: A therapy-based approach that responds to the impact of traumatic experiences in a way that avoids re-traumatization.

White Supremacy: The belief that the white race is inherently superior to other races and that white people should have control over people of other races. (Merriam-Webster)

ACKNOWLEDGMENTS

Pondering these acknowledgments have proven more challenging than writing the book. Although I risk missing someone who has contributed in some meaningful way, I offer the following acknowledgments with sincere appreciation and gratitude.

My agent, Mark Tauber, thank you for your persistence in contacting me and believing in my ability to write a book. Your guidance and insight have been invaluable. Truly, this book would not be here without you.

Joel Fotinos. I'm a novice to publishing, but throughout this process, I now realize the gift I've been given with you as my publisher. Thank you.

To Martin Quinn, John Karle, Emily Anderson, Sara Robb, and the design team, I'm grateful for your guidance, responsiveness, and enthusiasm for my heart's work. I'm forever grateful you all gave me such a gift for my first publishing experience. Because of your experience, professionalism, and attentiveness, this book was elevated to a level of quality that I could never have imagined. I'm honored to have journeyed with you to bring this book to life.

Rev. David Wallace and Rev. Martha Dewing, my deans at One Spirit Seminary, who encouraged me to embrace my gift of storytelling through writing. Thank you for believing in me when I didn't.

My steadfast and hardworking team that gave me the space I

needed to write this book by tending to social media and logistics, offering care to those needing spiritual care and standing sentry against the trolls who routinely flood our emails and comments with vitriol—much gratitude to Lynette, Stacey, and Afeni.

To my children—Lynette, Evan, and Byron. You got the broken parts of me. In spite of that, you became the beautiful, amazing humans you are today. I'm honored to be your mother.

To my brother and sister-in-law, David and Melissa, for rescuing me during one of the darkest times of my life. Without your help, my children and I would have been homeless, and my story would have ended much differently than here writing a book.

To my own mother, Karlene, who faced the challenges of single motherhood with courage and determination. I witnessed your collision with patriarchy so many times as you struggled to find work that paid a living wage. Without even knowing it, you were showing me what strong women can do when they believe in themselves. That courage and resilience resonates in the stories I share here. Thank you for never giving up. I'm glad you're my mama.

To the three friends and dog who I lost during the writing of this book—our stories may have ended, but the love you gave me and the sorrow I carry for each of you made me a better writer. So to Katrina, Dorothy, Rita, and Marmalade, thank you for seeing, believing, loving, and trusting me.

To my husband, John. For over thirty years we've journeyed together, enduring the inevitable and evolving to the determinable. The symmetry of our relationship is evidenced in the animals we've rescued, the benevolence we've extended to those in need, and the people to whom we've ministered. None of this happens without the teamwork and partnership that culminated from a commitment to do the right thing for our family and the world, borne out of a space of our love and commitment to each other. That symmetry is once again evident in a book that will hopefully inspire and help many. Thank you for believing in dreams and not believing me when I wanted to give up on those dreams.

NOTES

1. THE SPIRITUAL WILDERNESS

1. John of the Cross, *Dark Night of the Soul*, trans. Mirabai Starr (New York: Riverhead Books, 2003).
2. John of the Cross, *Dark Night*, 10.

2. EMOTIONAL FALLOUT

1. My spiritual journey invites me to still capitalize Jesus's pronouns. This is personal preference and should be considered only that. Each person should reflect on their own beliefs and values and consider how best to use language to describe their spiritual path and truths.

3. PATRIARCHY "MANSPLAINED"

1. Dictionary.com, s.v. "patriarchy," accessed August 1, 2023, https://www.dictionary.com/browse/patriarchy.
2. Bart Ehrman, "Why Women Came to Be Silenced," *Bart Ehrman Blog*, March 6, 2018, accessed August 5, 2023, https://ehrmanblog.org/why-women-came-to-be-silenced/.
3. "African-Americans in the American Workforce," U.S. Equal Employment Opportunity Commission, accessed August 5, 2023, https://www.eeoc.gov/special-report/african-americans-american-workforce.
4. Y. Hswen, F. Yang, C. Le-Compte, M. E. Hurley, H. Mattie, and T. T. Nguyen, "Structural Racism Through Sundown Towns and Its Relationship to COVID-19 Local Risk and Racial and Ethnic Diversity," *Preventive Medicine Reports* 35 (May 24, 2023): 102260, doi: 10.1016/j.pmedr.2023.102260.

5. "In U.S., Decline of Christianity Continues at Rapid Pace," Pew Research Center, accessed March 28, 2024, https://www.pewresearch.org/religion/2019/10/17/in-u-s-decline-of-christianity-continues-at-rapid-pace/.

6. "U.S. Church Membership Falls Below Majority for First Time," Gallup, accessed March 28, 2024, https://news.gallup.com/poll/341963/church-membership-falls-below-majority-first-time.aspx.

5. WHEN CHURCH HURTS

1. "In U.S., Decline of Christianity Continues at Rapid Pace," Pew Research Center, accessed March 28, 2024, https://www.pewresearch.org/religion/2019/10/17/in-u-s-decline-of-christianity-continues-at-rapid-pace/.

6. DISCOVERING THE DIVINE FEMININE

1. Expanding our language beyond just male and female to include nonbinary is important because it acknowledges and respects the diverse spectrum of gender and sexual identities, affirming the experiences and existence of individuals whose identities are fluid and extend beyond traditional binary categories.

2. Deuteronomy 32:11–12, 18; Psalms 131:2; Isaiah 42:14, 49:15; Hosea 11:3–4, 13:8; Matthew 23:37; Luke 13:34, 15:8–10.

3. Preston Ni, "The Impact of Gender Expectations on Boys and Young Men," *Psychology Today*, June 24, 2023, accessed November 25, 2023, https://www.psychologytoday.com/us/blog/communication-success/202306/the-impact-of-gender-expectations-on-boys-and-young-men.

4. Tzvi Freeman, "Who Is Shechinah, and What Does She Want from My Life?," Chabad.org, accessed November 28, 2023, https://www.chabad.org/library/article_cdo/aid/2438527/jewish/The-Shechina.htm.

5. Geoffrey W. Dennis, "What Is Kabbalah?," ReformJudaism.org, accessed November 28, 2023, https://reformjudaism.org/beliefs-practices/spirituality/what-kabbalah.

6. "Understanding Gender Identities," Trevor Project, August 23, 2021, accessed November 30, 2023, https://www.thetrevorproject.org/resources/article/understanding-gender-identities/?gad_source=1&gclid=Cj0KCQiAgqGrBhDtARIsAM5s0_n-O8Ig_lbSR2kKkXZjZ8iyNkWdLrklRFxIgbzxQCtp9q0bcYFBYFIaAjazEALw_wcB.

7. RECONCILIATION

1. "Historians Say Inquisition Wasn't That Bad," *The Guardian*, accessed March 28, 2024, https://www.theguardian.com/world/2004/jun/16/artsandhumanities.internationaleducationnews.

2. "Were 50 Million People Really Killed in the Inquisition?," National Catholic Register, accessed March 28, 2024, https://www.ncregister.com/blog/were-50-million-people-really-killed-in-the-inquisition.

3. "Inquisition," History, accessed March 28, 2024, https://www.history.com/topics/religion/inquisition.

4. In my research, I routinely found information about the benefits of church-sponsored mission trips, primarily written by Christian-centric sources. There has been much pushback from host countries, with people arguing that mission trips, sometimes labeled as *voluntourism*, are culturally insensitive, perpetuate stereotypes, and impose foreign values on local communities. The economic impacts include volunteers taking roles that could provide income to locals and the idea that funds for these trips might be better spent directly supporting the community. Additionally, such trips may lack sustainability, with short-term projects not providing lasting benefits, and can inadvertently focus more on the volunteer's personal experience rather than genuinely serving the community's needs. I agree and intentionally left them off this list.

8. WHAT AM I GOING TO DO ABOUT JESUS?

1. Adyashanti, *Resurrecting Jesus: Embodying the Spirit of a Revolutionary Mystic* (Boulder, CO: Sounds True, 2016).

9. LIFE AFTER DECONSTRUCTING

1. "Transformed Nonconformist: A Sermon by Dr. Martin Luther King, Jr.," Transforming Center, accessed September 2023, https://transformingcenter.org/2016/01/transformed-nonconformist/.